A Third Place

Other Books by Bob Kunzinger

Out of Nowhere: Scenes from St. Petersburg
Prof: One Guy Talking
Penance
Meanwhile in Leningrad
Fragments: Flash Non-Fiction
Borderline Crazy: Essays
Blessed Twilight
Out of the Way: A Father and Son in Spain

A Third Place

Notes in Nature

Bob Kunzinger

MADVILLE
PUBLISHING
Lake Dallas, Texas

FIRST EDITION

Requests for permission to reprint material from this work should be
sent to:

> Permissions
> Madville Publishing
> P.O. Box 358
> Lake Dallas, TX 75065

Acknowledgements:

Portions of the following writings have appeared either in whole or in
part in the following publications:
*A View from This Wilderness, The Washington Post, Kestrel: A Journal
of Literature and Art, Southern Humanities Review, The Virginian
Pilot, Connotation Press, Muse/A Journal.*

Cover Art: Mikel Wintermantel C.M.
Cover Design: Nancy Parsons
Author Photo: Michael Kunzinger

ISBN: 978-1-948692-16-8 paperback, 978-1-948692-17-5 ebook
Library of Congress Control Number: 2019937656

Look deep into nature, and then
you will understand everything better.

—Albert Einstein

Table of Contents

Part One

Transitions

Part Two

Part One

A Third Place

I've not come upon many places in my travels that simply don't change. Old neighborhoods seem smaller, the trees suffocate the once wide-open fields, and old hangouts usually have new crowds, or shut down, weeds pushing through parking lot pavement, some windows broken and boarded near a rusted dumpster. Such is civilization in neglect.

Even most of nature can show signs of change. Forests give way to fires, or new growth simply pushes out old oaks, changing the landscape. Rivers erode at the banks, and while the mountains can retain their majesty, trails and roads can rip small scars across the land, or some new cabin is built whose windows catch the sun and the glare flickers across the valley.

But I can stand on the sand behind the pier and know what I'm going to see when I look out over the water. Certainly, some days are rougher than others, and in winter a white foam can gather at the break point, but it is the same as it ever has been. The strength of a wave is like no other natural force on earth. Just to stand in the surf waist deep is a lesson in mobility and resistance no physics class can replicate. At some point you give in and fall back or dive forward, and feel that dark, salty, always slightly cool water sweep across every aspect of your body.

This is my other home. This is my third place.

We all should discover somewhere else. We have home, which comes with it certain responsibilities and routines. We have work with its predictable patterns of give and take. But we need a location that is neither, that is ours to claim how we want, and gather with friends, or be alone, and let our stresses and expectations dilute in the deluge of "somewhere else." For many it is a bar, or a coffee shop, or a park or a gym. For me, it's outside, on the sand, looking out toward Portugal, toward Spain, and Africa. Looking up the coast and wondering if anyone I used to know is looking south.

We all need a third place. For me, it is the wilderness, which, as Edward Abbey points out, is not a luxury but a necessity of the human spirit.

We all need somewhere that gets in our blood.

Moving On

We canoed yesterday up a small tributary where we paddled to the low-tide flats and eventually to a small swampy area near a farm. Along the way abundant osprey moved from branches to docks and back while several gulls stood their ground on pilings closer to the river. By the time we worked our way back to open water the current had increased so that we paddled much harder and gained less distance. In fact, we stayed against the strong current all the way back toward the bay.

We didn't take pictures; all we brought was water and peanut butter sandwiches. I never bring a phone. If we capsized or otherwise tumbled into the water, nothing would be lost, except us, possibly. It was very freeing and relaxing, of course. We spent a good part of the morning drifting past large embankments with old houses set back. Each has an extensive dock reaching to the channel, and some homes are so hidden by trees it was only the sun hitting the windows that made me realize a house was on the hill at all. Further along, the shrinking creek moved toward corn and soybean fields, so we turned around and worked against the rising tide. At one point a tern plummeted into the water exactly in front of us stealing away with a small croaker.

We've paddled along these small creeks and the wide river right at the mouth of the bay for twenty years now.

Sometimes we bring food and something to drink and we'll rest on the beaches of one of the islands and have lunch then collect sea-worn oyster and scallop shells. When I was in high school we had a canoe and explored the shores of another river years before development turned the riverbank into a suburb. Back then I'd often bring a book to read and let myself drift in an inlet. Sometimes a fish would jump and slap the side of the aluminum boat. Those waters and these, about seventy-five nautical miles apart, are fantastically similar in their vistas, tides, and even their life; both are a source of oysters, crabs, and small fish. In both cases it was a short distance from the inlet to the bay, and in both cases I preferred not to bring anything along.

These days I'm hauling even less. Today we left behind the weight of negative thought from the media. I left behind the comments of politicians, the commentary of news hawks, the criticism of the swarming public. I consciously left behind fears of nuclear war and domestic terrorism. Leaving it all behind is what happens in this place, in this wilderness. Most people tell me they'd have no problem leaving the phone in the car, step aside for a few hours and see how far they can drift away from the tethered world. I believe them, of course, but they don't do it. And the lack of purity in our lives is exactly what is missing. We live in a blended world now where work follows us home and keeps us company through the night, where weekends are spent grading papers or reading rough drafts online, or checking spreadsheets after Sunday breakfast, or talking at half-time to bosses or interns about what didn't get done or needs to get done.

When my father was a stockbroker on Wall Street and took the train home on Friday, there was a complete disconnect until Monday from that world. If the rotary phone rang and he answered it, before the caller got to the reason for the interruption, there would be several minutes of apologies for bothering him while at home with his family.

The arguments for getting work done at home are clear, but just as clear is the dilution which accompanies such compromise. The purity of being present, the singleness of existing in one place, is evaporating.

So I opted out of bringing along piles of work papers, my to-do list around the house, and any concerns I have had about food. I just pushed off and paddled back. I love the art of canoeing. The very nature of moving forward through the water demands I sweep the engulfing waters behind me. In fact, the river and bay have enough information already to occupy my continuing curiosity about time. Just a few miles to the south is an underwater crater where some long-ago meteor helped form the east coast. And throughout the bay and river are reefs of shipwrecks hundreds of years old, lost during storms while exploring the wilds of these now domesticated shores. Out there we are constantly reminded of the fragility of time and the futile pursuit of hurtful, damaging, misplaced energy.

I can clear my head while out on the river. I can remind myself that nature is the best example of how if all is ever lost, one of our strongest traits is the ability to start again. It helps in times like these to know that no matter how bad things might seem, we can adjust our course, and if we tack correctly, we can even move with grace against the current problems. Thoreau's thoughts ring true in these times: In the wilderness is the salvation of the world.

This morning we saw a man at a boat slip, alone, returning his small fishing boat to the trailer behind his truck. It took him just minutes and then he was off. He hadn't caught anything, but he waved with the pleasure of a man who had just completely let go of whatever might have weighed him down. I was never a fisherman, but right then I knew I would be good at it since catching anything is not really required. I would do as well as Thoreau, who wrote, "Many men go fishing all their lives without knowing it is not fish they are after."

I am not trying to hide; I am not paddling away from anything. I am moving into the permanence which is nature as I did forty years ago, as I hope to do for years to come. It doesn't ridicule; it doesn't pass judgement. It doesn't change the rules or tease or taunt. And while it can be brutal, it is brutally honest. And when I again navigate those waters and can deliberately move through the day, I will be, like Thoreau, ready to return to civilization.

If God Agrees

Six swans have made their home here at the river. I saw them last night for the first time and then this morning. The water today is still, like glass, like ice, and looks more an inverted sky than brackish river-water.

My son says the swans have been there for a week or more. I hope they're here to stay, at least a while, but more likely they have been fooled by the warm temperatures—in the seventies—and are headed north. Soon they'll reach the Southern Tier of New York where the weather is not so kind right now, and turn around, questioning their internal clocks. And osprey, too, glide from the duck pond a mile and a half across the river. Osprey are abundant here on the bay, but not now; not yet. Usually we are still graced with bald eagles, which don't get along with osprey, and so they somehow split the seasons between them.

I stood a long time and watched the swans, listened to one of them hiss, the water quietly lapping at the rocks and sand. I want to appreciate them as long as I can. I was relieved they were still there this morning. I'm sure before long they'll be gone, and who knows which one of us will not be here next year. I'm plagued with persistent thoughts of "enjoy this while you can, you never know." I think that comes from my maternal grandmother whom every time I would say "Talk to you soon, Grandma" to on the phone would answer, "God willing." I laughed back then.

Nothing is promised, nothing guaranteed, no matter how safe we play it, no matter how predictable seem the persistent patterns of our lives. This is why I take long walks along the river and bay. What is there now may be lost or may leave, or I may grow tired of the work necessary to stroll along a path or the sand. In art, I am always grateful for the likes of Fra Angelica, Monet, Sisley, Rodin, and more. They used their talents as they should to isolate time and pass it on to us, centuries and millennia later. We can stare at the work of the good Dominican painter and see the beauty of his subject matter, of course, but also see the 15th century, the European sentiment, the philosophical bend, the life of then. So too in nature, if we understand the temporal state of such perennial lives.

I watched the swans and recognized the extremes in my world. There is the art of it, for example, made permanent by artists such as Thomas Cole and Mikel Wintermantel, whose landscape paintings fill our souls with such calmness. They bring instant peace of mind as well as transport us to pastoral locales. But there is also the temporal reality of it, as moments pass, as loved ones pass, as we age and realize the greatest treasures can't be recreated by the most talented of artists, or often, for some of us, even simply remembered—only experienced, now. Right now.

The swan spends her life hissing. It is a gentle sound, almost as if she is trying to harmonize with the water or the soft breezes through the reeds along the shoreline. But right before she dies she lets out a long, serene call, just before the end, as if to offer us one last beautiful moment before she leaves us for good.

It is, quite literally, her swan song.

Sometimes when my mind is clear and I'm not distracted by the give and take of going and coming back, I can sense every aspect of nature in the constant call of its own swan song. It is then that I am inspired to do the same, to stop hissing and make every call as beautiful as I can, even if I do wake up ready to try it again the next day. It is how I wish I could be all the time, to bring as much beauty as I can, to see as much beauty as I can, as often as I can. And then tomorrow—God willing—do it again.

A Visceral Life

Maybe (maybe) the most universal affective aspect of life is weather. It concerns every person who wakes and must go outside, and even those who remain cloistered. It determines what we wear, how we travel, what grows and can be harvested, what we eat, our health, our heating bills, flight schedules, road conditions, skin cancer, landscaping, pizza delivery, getting to work, to school, to the stores to buy food, to our friends and family in need. To be clear—it is everywhere, this weather.

No metaphors here. No convoluted comparisons. Just weather.

I love to walk in the rain. Part of that is I know when I'm done I can dry off, change my clothes and make some tea. It is the same with snow. The cold tightness of my skin on a blustery winter day feels oddly healthy, as does the blistering sun on my neck in August. I love wearing my flip flops, shorts, a t-shirt and sweating profusely as the hours pass well into the afternoon while walking in the sun, listening to nature react. Equally, I'm completely engaged when I must put on three shirts, a hoodie, sweatpants and two pairs of socks just to be able to go for a walk during which I might see deer, cardinals, and various other life scooting around for something to eat while I am engulfed in the deafening silence of the snow. I'll cover the porch rail with seed and stay dressed and sit on the porch. Those birds don't care that I'm a foot away; they stay, they brave my presence. Only in winter.

Then I go back inside and change into warm sweatpants and have tea. See, it works for me; it doesn't work if you have no home. A little perspective there. Every time I walk in extreme weather I think about someone who might be in the streets of some cold place, or blistering hot place, and I remind myself it is more than bearable for a little while until I make the choice some can't—to get out of the weather.

"Come in from the cold," people say. "No, I can't go with you while it is pouring out," people say. "Wow, it is just too damn hot," people say.

They're not speaking for me. I'm more in tune with John Ruskin who said there is really no such thing as bad weather, only different kinds of good weather.

I like to spend as much time as possible immersed in the unbearably brilliant sensual joy of that weather. That includes rainy days. There are times, of course, the weather seems not so much part of nature as it is simply nature having a bad spell. Blizzards, tornadoes, drought; these to me are nature's way of hemorrhaging. Van Gogh wrote, "There is peace even in the storm." I understand that. When it rains hard or the wind is fierce and I can hear branches snap, as long as I am safe it all simply reminds me I am alive to experience this weather, this turn of currents, this atmospheric screwball, and I feel somehow calmer and more alive.

I prefer perfect weather, the still day with low humidity and pleasant sunshine. But equally, to experience the rain on my face, getting drenched, reaching out and being a part of the earth and nature instead of it simply being something "around" me or something "outside," floods my senses and elevates my awareness to keep everything else in perspective. Who among us during the calm days doesn't hope for some metaphoric lottery win, some breakthrough in life to make us feel like there is something more to grab on to? And then severe weather arrives, and we shift our thoughts and pray no one gets hurt and our property is spared, and above all else that we come out of it alive.

When some system swirls off the African coast and creeps its way up the Saffir-Simpson Scale, it throws our lives into a whirlwind of measuring value and understanding perspective to discover what is essential. Hell, just a little rain should do the same thing. Putting on warm clothes and having tea is more enjoyable when doing so is preceded by a good drenching. The problem is clear, however: people prefer those conditions which remain unnoticeable, the Goldilocks' Syndrome of not wishing to tolerate or endure or experience. Many wish to simply be, without definition or subjectivity. No storms, please. No.

The weather is constantly changing, and so are we. Rachel Carson believed that a rainy day was the perfect time to walk in the woods. Of course. And the "best thing to do when it is raining," Longfellow tells us, "is to let it rain."

Longfellow's Rain

Yes, I like the rain. Always have. I like the way I am completely aware of the here and now when I'm outside, blinking away the dripping wet from my face. One time, just east of Fisterra, Spain, my son and I walked all morning and afternoon in a steady downpour. We were drenched and walked along muddy trails for miles and miles. Some paths ran through trees and it wasn't all that bad, and sometimes we found refuge, like under the overhang of a medieval church, another time in a pub where we played foosball and had a drink. We had no plans, weren't going anywhere except farther east on our way back from the end of the earth. And anyway, we knew already that eventually that evening when we changed, our clothes would dry. What's the big deal?

When I was a child and went for bike rides on Saturday afternoons after it rained, a streak of puddle-wet would whip up my back. And while it was slightly irritating if a pebble took flight with the water, it was also visceral, absolute; the rain drowned out any sense of shadows from earlier or later, allowed only the present to persist. Sometimes my face was so wet my skin softened.

It is raining now, and I am aware of how much I can feel it on my skin when I think about how my father no longer can; my father and so many friends we've lost by now, some not far from here. Or how my friends so far away might be inside working, looking outside glad they are not out in the rain. I picture the times when I had to find my way through a small village and it was raining, and I didn't mind at all. It is reassuring when I remember those times. It makes me realize no matter what, I will always be fine, always be okay. If I can be completely at peace while walking in the rain, why would I ever let anything else bother me?

Another time in Spain Michael and I walked up a long road in the rain and an elderly man was standing in his doorway and asked us to come inside. He made us coffee and gave us some bread and we sat inside awhile, grateful for the break, more grateful for talking to someone new. The rain often brings people together, sometimes in doorways, sometimes in sandwich shops, and sometimes on grassy paths in some third place.

It seems more and more we are less aware of the here and now, but weather keeps us in the moment. It is a subtle reminder that nature is in control; the wilderness will win eventually. I love standing back to watch it all. I love the way I can still feel the rain on my face, or the sun pressing on my neck on a July afternoon. Or the snow and a cool wind coming down from the north in November, when being outside takes some presence of mind.

Let the rain kiss you
Let the rain beat upon your head with silver liquid drops
Let the rain sing you a lullaby
The rain makes still pools on the sidewalk
The rain makes running pools in the gutter
The rain plays a little sleep song on our roof at night
And I love the rain.

April Rain Song
−Langston Hughes

Lecture

Before we slip into the nature and the nurture of now, a quick lecture from an aging professor-turned-pilgrim:

What if one day you left your phone at home and went for a long walk? Would you wonder if everything is okay? Would you keep touching your pockets, looking behind you? At the very least would you wonder the time? How long, I wonder, before you turned and went home to check your texts, your messages. You're hooked—we all are.

But what if one day you just keep walking. Not many people anymore remember what it was like to have no ability to call home anytime they wanted. We looked for payphones at gas stations. And when we finished plugging it with coins for the three minutes we bought to talk, it was barely long enough to say, "Great, everything's going great! How is everyone? Good! Okay, I'll talk to you next week!"

Next week. Sometimes, next month. It is in part how we grew up, and it most definitely is how we matured. But those three minutes, then, was enough to know everyone was fine and we could focus on what was happening around us. We were fully aware of place. We kept no records. We didn't update anyone. No texts. No tweets. No snapshots. We were that rare state of being which is slipping into the past: solely and completely in the moment.

No phone, no internet, no messages, no voicemail, no apps, no games, no kidding—just conversation with whomever you're with or whoever happens along. If you wanted a picture of yourself at some site, or with a friend, you stopped someone walking by and asked that person to take it—we didn't have long sticks to hold the 35mm. But that person would be friendly, and conversations would ensue, and information about local places to eat or drink could be discovered. We don't do that now—we are in such a selfie world we don't risk much beyond the length of our arms. Am I the only one who misses the long talks and laughter after not seeing someone for a few days and "catching up"?

I do understand the obsession with photographs. They make me miss that time I was twenty-five and sitting on a couch, laughing; and they make me wish we had hundreds of more pictures of then, of the endless laughter of then, of the immeasurable hope of then. Yet they remind me how we were in that moment; too much, in fact, to spend any time trying to capture that moment. We were too busy living it.

But back to that long walk: At the end of that long day if you did just keep walking, by bedtime, phoneless, you might miss your normal routine to lie on your back, phone in hand, and seek out information for a while. You can't, though, because you're tech-less, and you can't imagine that you ever couldn't, but you do. No worries, the world keeps spinning, friends are not diligently waiting to hear from you or have anything to report, and the news is not going away.

The next morning is harder still. You ache to know what happened overnight about which you have no information all these hours later. Did someone text? Call? It's killing you, but you can't go back now. You've walked too far. The anxiety, withdrawal, is real and stressful, and like giving up a blanket or a bottle, each step seems endless, the day an eternity. You want to borrow someone's phone. You want to just check real fast—find out everything is fine. And what if you did? Everything is fine, benign, most likely predictable and familiar. We crave the familiar and predictable; it falsely makes us feel safer. It is why we stay in bad relationships which become routine; it is why we stay in bad jobs which have no future but which we've mastered and manipulated.

I know the arguments. The advances in this world have made much of our lives infinitely more convenient than then. No contest, and I am often thrilled that I can be a part of "what's next" as we bullet toward tomorrow. But there is a price to pay—there is always a tradeoff—and as far as some technology is concerned that price is how you spend your time. Thirty years will pass faster than you can fathom, trust me. Don't spend it looking down.

Here's a test to see if your priorities are in order: plan to travel for a week and tell everyone you know you will be out of touch the entire time—no calls, no texts, no emails, no matter what happens. Tell them you'll check in when you're back to make sure your loved ones are alive; otherwise, you'll be meeting new people, finding cafés and maybe a motel where you'll spend nights drinking wine and laughing with new friends from new places, and you'll catch the sunrise without capturing it on camera. No one needs to know what's going on; they'll ask when you return. No one needs to be updated, see pictures, videos, receive OMG texts at every mountain and mystery along the way. They'll ask when you get home.

You're without your umbilical, untethered, freefalling into yourself absent of the consistent clicks and taps of that certain cell. We grow anxious when faced with our own thoughts without possible deflection, no technological tangent. But the anxiousness erodes, and new conversations linger like lace curtains, sometimes lifting, often drifting down and raised only by the occasional wistful comment, and it is peaceful. You had forgotten "peaceful." You maybe never learned just how to be full of peace.

But it isn't so silent, is it, this peacefulness? This ironic disconnection links you to those nearby, connects you with others who make eye contact, talk about the places they've been, talk about the possibilities. Talk about unplugged! Most of the time you talk about life and how far you might reach, and the truth is you can't reach out and grasp something if you're holding anything. We do that though, we want to reach for more but not let go of what we've got. "If I put this down," we say, "I might lose touch with what I know." We haven't yet realized Shakespeare's decree that "one touch of nature makes the whole world kin."

Take a deep breath. Take a moment. Take, for instance, that time you sat by the water at the north end of the beach and a couple caught you staring at the trees near the houses and they told you of an area filled with Spanish moss over walking trails just a few miles off the ocean. "Lived here for eighteen years," you say, "And never knew that." If you were looking down, they never would have said a thing. You know they wouldn't. But the absence of such a small device can dial up the most spontaneous connections.

Really, you get used to this simplicity, this absence of noise, of interruption, of course you do. Find out what it is like to walk with empty hands and touch the world, what it is like to listen to nothing at all. At night those hands hold wine and bread and you hear tales of the day. We tell stories out loud, and we listen to stories and share moments, out loud, and we live, as much as possible, out loud. In this way, every single conversation is different. Every single shared sunset is different. And we come to have a sense of the senses.

And we learn, eventually we learn, the most important moments cannot, cannot, cannot be captured by the most efficient technology. Sometimes you need to be away from someone to understand just how close you really are.

A Lesson in Centering

Winter at night in the country is silent. To the north is a harvested field where often geese land just around dusk, and in the river beyond that. Just on the east is the bay, and there's nothing but trees to the west and south. When the sky is clear this time of year it is cold, and now Saturn is settling below the horizon just after midnight. The just-about-to-be-Super Full Moon is climbing over the Chesapeake, and if it weren't so bright the Milky Way in the south would be more visible. This is the way it is; this is seven at night in the country in winter.

This is the Cold Moon. It is the first full moon in winter, so the Cold Moon. In two weeks is the geminid meteor shower offering more than one hundred and twenty flybys an hour. If you lay on your back on a blanket in the grass in the country in December, you can probably make a few wishes every minute.

After a while we'll heat up some cider, and I'll start a fire in the fire pit on the patio near the back path. I am sure that while we will enjoy ourselves, we both would liked to have been in New York City, with family, walking.

Honestly, our lives should revolve around family. Unfortunately, too often that is not the way it is. We battle with deadlines and struggle against the proverbial sand seeping through the hourglass. I would like to slow the whole thing down. I'd love to be able to live like we lived half a century ago when cousins were a stone's-throw away and every day someone was around, sharing dinner, and we would run into each other at the stores. That was the nature of things; that was the nurturing we knew. Now we are scattered like stars and to meet with more than a handful of us means mapping out distances to common locales, coordinating schedules, and planning ahead for accommodations and flights. The simplicity of saying, "Hey, we're going to get a fire going in the pit tonight, drink some wine and use the telescope; why don't you come by," has receded to so long ago I barely remember when. I wouldn't change much about my life; but if I could make one small adjustment, I'd arrange it for all my cousins and extended family to live nearby, especially my siblings and their families. I suppose we appreciate each other more for the lack of constant contact and the possibilities of "next time." But part of me wishes to put that to the test.

Still, without family around, few events bring me more peace than sitting outside with my adult son, having cider and looking for constellations in the night sky. It is incomprehensible how much space exists between us and the stars, and how long it would take to get there. When the world is too much with us, we can always find a little peace out in the field in the perfect stillness of night and watch some meteor shoot by, dimmed only by the light of the moon.

Sometimes I simply look toward Vega or Orion, or I get lost in the Pleiades. It is silent out here stretching clear across the water, and the chill reaches deep inside, and you realize this is exactly how it was for Copernicus, for Galileo, for our grandfathers, and forever it will be exactly like this. And you realize life should always be like this, but it is inexpressible, so you look around for someone to share it with, because talking about it falls short, is incomplete.

And you realize right then that family is the center, the absolute center of your universe. At some point we come to understand that life revolves around them.

Sitting This One Out

I sit in my green writing chair my father gave me years ago and look past my books and paintings into the wilderness which surrounds my home. The birds could not find food in the morning's snow so a slow spread of seed across the porch rails brought nature as close as possible without opening the windows. House wrens, warblers, robins, cardinals, downy woodpeckers and others all winged in from the apple trees to the rail, grabbed some seeds or stood and ate them there. Next to the porch is a larger than me thorn bush covered in red leaves which the birds use for hiding. They popped in and out from the bush to the porch and back to grab more of the only food around. Eventually they all work their way back to the woods by dodging from tree to tree like soldiers moving forward on a night raid. The thorn bush first, of course, followed by a quick flight to the first holly. From there the apple trees, despite their dormant branches, are fine for resting because of the snowy limbs. The last leg is a short one to more holly at the edge of the woods. Once there they seem to pause, look back as if they are wondering if they had enough, or if they forgot anything, and then they disappear into the high branches of dense forest. Later they'll return.

I have found two ways to experience nature. First by moving through her: Sunday drives, evening strolls, afternoon hikes, morning runs, and any average commute. We take in what we can, view the variety of colors in spring and the fall foliage. But I've driven the route to work enough times in two decades to not see it at all anymore. Are the trees taller? I assume they must be, but a change cannot be noticed by one who watches it grow. I cross three bridges along the way and two of them have been rebuilt since I started. Still, my mind is elsewhere when nature exists sixty-five miles an hour slower than me. We can't always be aware of nature; I understand this. But I'm not fully sure I know what it is that distracts me to begin with.

There are other means to move through nature: A few years ago, my son and I trained across the vast empire of eastern Russia, across the steppes and hills of Siberia, and to the Pacific Coast. Along the way we saw thousands of acres of birch forests and hundreds of small, curious shacks all painted royal blue. I could never drive across Siberia, so the train would have to do, but the journey left me with more questions than answers. Who works out there? Are the dilapidated gulags we passed empty or just in ruins? What kinds of wildlife did we pass, mostly at night, just beyond the trees away from the tracks? Surely a tiger or two stood and watched us roll along.

As if extremes exemplified my existence, the following summer we walked the medieval pilgrimage route from southern France to Santiago, Spain, on the Camino de Santiago. The Camino is five hundred miles long, and at just about three miles an hour or so means every Basque slug, meseta insect and Galician fly could be personally experienced and known by name. We watched the colors of the sky change and stood still every few kilometers to take in the vistas, drink some coffee, and walk the rocky paths again. To drive that distance takes roughly eight hours. It took us five weeks. One sees more when moving slowly. It is simple physics. But in the end we are still moving through. Nature does not hurry, says Lao Tzu, yet everything is accomplished.

Which leads me to the second way to experience nature: sit still.

Birds tilt their heads when they eat, as if they can't see the food unless their eyes face down. Most varieties get along well, but the chickadees are little bastards. They'll chase away or dare anyone, squirrels included. Yellow warblers are neurotic, and cardinals look pissed off though I think they just want to be left alone, like old writers.

I can't remember the last time I simply stared at the bare brown branches against the gray sky. Somehow the white snow on dark green holly leaves brings the yard to life. I have lived in this wilderness for twenty years but each time I look out the window is as if I never before sat and stared at trees, at birds' wings just inches away, at the patches of green grass surrounded by a dusting of snow. Usually in spring we pay attention to the trees, when bare branches give way to buds, which give way to new life. Or in the autumn when we calculate our driving times on Sunday afternoons for when the leaves will be at their "peak."

I sat perfectly still one Sunday, doused in the narration-free documentary playing out before me and discovered something phenomenal: trees are *always* at their peak.

They stand strong like church steeples. The thick brown branches reach up, shirts off, muscles taut, every bone exposed, wrestling, bent at the elbows, visible like some skeleton x-ray against a low, gray sky, or a deep dark blue sky, or a snowy dirty white sky, and these trees don't balk, they don't flinch, and the colors never seem to start or finish; there are no lines, as Manet noticed, "only areas of color, one against another." These trees dare every aspect of deep winter weather. The wind moves through unnoticed, and snow catches crevices and freezes further growth for months. What wonder it is to watch their stern and steady rise, proof of decades, sometimes centuries, dug in for winter, standing guard in forests and backyards, unable for a while to block the sun, bare enough for us to listen at night to the geese. Starlings settle on naked limbs, thousands of starlings like leaves land, rest awhile, then leave, the trees once again alone waiting out winter, as if to say they'll let winter leave when they're damn well ready, and while they may not appear "perfect," in nature, everything is perfect writes Alice Walker. "Trees can be contorted, bent in weird ways, and they're still beautiful."

I used to think time went by so fast. I remember my dad sitting on the porch in our backyard watching birds outside. He was a relatively quiet man but loved to watch the birds. One time he and my mom watched a pair of cardinals teach their young one to fly. They watched it fail a few times until it finally took to the air, making it to the nearest branch, not far from the porch. I never had time for that when I lived there. I wonder if my parents, maybe like the cardinals themselves, were both thrilled to see me leave the nest but sad at how fast I found my wings. Now I sit in his chair watching a robin work through the seed on the rail, and I realize it isn't time that moves too fast, it's me.

Too Early for the Sun

The earth was frozen here this morning, and as I walked along the sand at the ocean's edge, I didn't leave footprints. I moved along as if on pavement, and so I moved along quite a while despite the freezing temperatures and the winds from the northwest. The water was relatively calm, and it seemed almost an effort for the waves to run too far past the break. A few fishing boats moved out from the inlet, and several dolphins barely broke the surface fifty yards out.

This is my constant. This is any time of my life standing here in December watching some planet just above the horizon dim then fade to a brightening sky.

We are inundated with information, and most of it is negative, or contradictory, or frightening, or simply pathetic. From presidential tweets to congressional shenanigans, to civil-war-like partisanship, to murders and terrorism, to racism and hypocritical judgements; to financial fears for graduate students, middle class workers, young graduates, seniors on fixed incomes; to the awakening of brave women exposing the horrific trend in society of men—particularly those in positions of power—to blatantly or subtly offend others. My mind is saturated with information, and little of it is positive, none of it is healthy.

Worst of all is the backstabbing and lies.

And it is so easy, so very methodical, to stand and take it, absorb the superfluous energy, allow ourselves to be saturated in the useless and the pointless. "What a tragedy," people say when someone has a nervous breakdown or a stroke, or simply can't shake the depressive funk which settles on shoulders like ash. But the true tragedy is how simple it is to just step away, simply step away, yet people don't. Not for good, of course, not for long enough to put careers or family or grades in jeopardy. No, just a quick step away, briefly, to stand again in the very essence of some place away from such claustrophobic ways.

What a hell of a race. Honestly, I simply cannot wrap my head around how a species with such potential can be so destructive on so many levels, from ridicule to greed to mass annihilation. What the hell happened? Really, if God's coming back, now's good. Is God already here? I hope not; I truly would be quite disappointed to know that. I prefer this mess we have made is all from free will. I can believe in that. This is the most likely scenario since there doesn't appear to be a plan, does there?

I understand this is an oversimplified view of world events and situations, and to "step away" is an idealistic reaction concerning what we are capable of. In fact, it crosses decidedly into triteness. But one of the tenants of productive human behavior is to surround yourself with positive people, to step away from the negative ones, the complainers. To remain healthy, creative people should engage with other creative types, and planners and visionaries should be working toward new advances with other like-minds. Of course. But these like-minded individuals are getting harder to find, harder to recognize for the cloud of unknowing coming from the media, from the meetings, from the droves of people speaking out of both sides of their mouths. But Terry Tempest Williams nailed it when she wrote, "Wildness reminds us what it means to be human, what we are connected to rather than what we are separate from."

That's when, early, very early in the morning before the sun has clawed its way to the horizon, I step off the boardwalk and move to the waves which don't make it much past the break, and the sand is firm like pavement, and my feet don't even leave imprints. A cold wind comes from the northwest and keeps me decidedly in the moment. It all seems predetermined out there. When was the last time you went for a walk outside in very cold weather? Not to the car, or from the car to the mall. I mean a walk without destination, absent of headlines and voting results. It is the ultimate in the immediate; it remains the only evidence of permanence I can find, yet our opportunities to engage in such permanence seem so fleeting. Even Steinbeck, whom I'm sure I would get along with famously, wrote, "Time is more complex near the sea than in any other place, for in addition to the circling of the sun and the turning of the seasons, the waves beat out the passage of time."

Out on the horizon this morning, well before the sun broke through, some thin clouds ran the length to the right like jib sails running out front heading to the Outer Banks just to the south. The water was warmer than the air, and sea birds kept diving by me hoping I had food as I walked. One landed near my feet disturbing a few sandpipers I was sneaking past.

The pier is closed for the season, and the lights running down the boardwalk were still on so I could clearly see no one was around but a few military personnel out for an early run. One old man wrapped tight in a parka walked his dog.

But at the water's edge all I could hear was water, and even that so gently I could sometimes also hear the dolphins' fins break the surface. It was that calm. No hypocrisy. No backstabbing or negativity. It is the ultimate definition of truth. It remains the most honest experience possible.

Gravity

This morning I had breakfast on the pier probing out over the Atlantic. I had an omelet stuffed with scallops, crab-meat, shrimp and cheese, with toast and home fries. The sun skipped off the silvery, glass waves and the breezes kept the humidity at bay.

I was alone. It is still too early in the season for crowds, and I sat under an awning watching dolphins and pelicans work their way down the coast. I knew they'd reach the jetty at First Street and circle back. They always do.

The pier is probably twenty feet off the sand offering more of a crow's nest view of the horizon than a body-surfer's vantage. And as the water was unimposing, I drifted off into the distance, circumnavigating the globe in my mind as I have for decades. This morning I sat and stared at Portugal and the northwest coast of Spain.

Who hasn't stared out the window at work, at school, at home drifting as far away as possible from the demands and diversions of life? It is how I combat depression; it is how I combat the predictable.

This third place of mine can be expansive, but the "farther one gets into the wilderness," Teddy Roosevelt insisted, "the greater is the attraction of its lonely freedom." True.

I looked just below the sun toward what I knew is Galacia and pictured the people there right then, right at that moment, staring west across the Atlantic from Fisterra, where my son and I stood just a few years ago. Right over the curve of the earth, just time away, are villages still, with small cafés where pilgrims right now rest, as we did. If I had better eyesight and the ability to bend vision, I could be looking right at them. I *was* looking right at them except for the physics of it all.

And further south is West Africa, where I had ceeb—a rice dish—for the first time and talked to friends over Flagg Beer several decades ago. It is so easy to fall into the trap of remembering the "time" it was instead of the "place" it is. I'm sure some of my favorite spots have changed while others, like the tiny chicken villages of northern Spain, are the same as they always have been. But all of them are still right there nonetheless.

Don't we all have a tendency to braid time and place so they remain inextricable, when the truth is separating them might allow melancholy to become hope?

Perception forces us into believing that things close by are larger and more significant than things far away, even in time. Often it is just that life blocks our view. So I sat and stared not at the ocean as much as the unseen reality farther away than the stretches of my biological ability allows, and I realized again what a ride it has been on this spinning playground. I've been blessed to be able to see so much, and not by moving mountains or praying for miracles. I just decided to go. It is easy to forget that in the end the difference between when you dream about something and when you pursue that dream is a split second separated by the notion of simply deciding to do it.

These days the news has lost control and the information barrage is saturating our existence; but on the pier this morning I remembered how fragile and fleeting our time is that we waste so much of it tangled up in the goings and comings of the small tentacles of anger and negativity. For example, while drinking orange juice I looked just to the north, across the other side of the bar about four thousand miles toward Norway, where early every morning our neighbor, the fisherman Magnus, came back with a cod, cut out the liver for himself, and gave us the rest. On the other side of the fjord outside the kitchen window of our cabin was nothing for thousands of miles to the North Pole. I glanced that way this morning.

And I looked toward the piers on Long Island, the docks on Martha's Vineyard, the rivers and bays of New York. Sometimes I get tired and give in to the shadows, but every so often I stumble upon a morning like this and I have no trouble buying into Emmanuel Kant's insistence that "what's next" is entirely up to us.

Have you ever sat quietly on a balcony and gazed out on the ocean? Two ideas emerge. First, it pushes part of us toward the possibilities which we are afraid to say out loud, and nearly simultaneously forces the lesser angels off our shoulders, where we sweep them away with the ridiculous minutia.

Sometimes it seems as if it would be better to crawl back into the cave. So many people in these days of political uncertainty and cultural dehydration seem to be staring at shadows again, looking away from the flames, obsessed with the flickering of residual data on the walls. The tragedy, of course, is the fire will burn out and the shadows are an illusion. The only course of action is to see what's out there, but too often we stand in the doorway, hesitant, terrified by terrorism and insecure about disconnection.

We miss everything because we are scared we might miss something.

The server refilled my coffee two times. The sun moved above a cloudbank and warmed the pier and the sand, and tourist kids from further north gathered along the waterline. I haven't been that quiet in a long time. Sometimes at night, but never at that hour of the morning. I watched the silvery reflection on the waves and then glanced up at the sun, our very own star, no telescope necessary, and remembered all the times I watched the sunrise or set at various places fore and aft, from Arizona to the Sea of Japan. It feels good sometimes to stop and remind myself that I couldn't find my way back to the cave if I tried.

The First Sign of Light

We looked at the stars again. I don't know their names and no matter how many times I read about them or someone explains them to me, that part of my brain simply doesn't operate well. I know Orion because of the old Orion Motion Pictures; that's it. It is the same part of the brain that doesn't allow me to remember names of students or meeting times. But out under the stars on a clear cold night you really don't need to know the names of anything, not the stars, not students, not the days of the week or the towns on a map. It is late, and you're outside like our primitive ancestors stood outside, and there are stars, the exact stars our original DNA saw, and labels are useless, except to call them timeless, to call them exquisite, and to know that they are.

Some nights the temperatures are freezing, but that is usually because of no haze or cloud cover so the stars are even more brilliant. With the small scope we can see the rings of Saturn and four of Jupiter's moons. We have also seen Venus and Mars, and a herd of constellations that start with a P or a C, I forget. One of them is Pleiades, I know that. They are the seven sisters.

I do know the Big Dipper when I see it, and a long time ago I saw the Southern Cross on a continent far away. I assume the brightest star I see so often in the west is either Alpha Centauri or Vega, but I really don't care one way or the other. I'm not going there, not teaching astronomy, and I'm not trying to impress anyone at all. I did take an astronomy class in college, and on one cold night we took a powerful telescope to a hillside and took turns scanning the sky. When it was my turn I said, "This is out of focus; it's all fuzzy," to which the professor looked and exclaimed, "Holy Cow, you found a nebula!" He then told me I didn't discover one but I did point the telescope toward a fuzzy patch someone else had discovered. Still, I'm not unromantic—I wasn't oblivious to the idea that I was staring deep into space, across billions of years ago toward eternities from now.

I can't wait for clear nights at home when we can see stars in the darkness across the bay or the river, but what I enjoy looking at the most is the moon. I never tire of staring at the craters, especially when it is a half-moon, which makes the craters so much easier to see than when the moon is full. My son will point the telescope toward Saturn's rings or Jupiter's moons and I'll say, "Yeah, nice, now let's look at our moon again." He always obliges, but I understand why it isn't as important to him as it is me.

In the late sixties I was just another kid like so many caught up in the space race, following the Apollo missions as they came close to the moon, orbiting it, sending back images of its surface. I had a brown jacket with a NASA patch sewed on the sleeve and an American flag on the other. I knew every aspect of space travel—the speed needed to exit the earth's gravitational pull, how the Saturn V rocket was built, the space inside, the Space outside, the purpose of each mission, and the names of every single astronaut.

I turned nine in July of '69 and we just moved into our new home. I remember my sister sitting on the floor and I joined her as we watched Walter Cronkite dictate the actions of Neil Armstrong and Buzz Aldrin while Michael Collins orbited above them. The next evening, I remember going outside and looking up at the sky, knowing they were up there and wanting more than anything to go there someday. We then lived in a world where we had walked on the moon. Incredible. It was the first serious ambition I remember; I wanted to train at NASA and be an astronaut. Of course. It wasn't because I liked the science. It was because I liked the ambition of it all, the pursuit of something seemingly impossible, literally otherworldly. Even at nine it meant to me that despite the turmoil of the sixties we kept our eye on the ball and refused to believe we could not achieve Kennedy's decree. I am not sure the succeeding generations have a comparable ambition, at least not one as grand. Mars? Someday. Not yet.

So we go out and look at the stars and the full moon, and whenever I do I have hope again, despite the problems with the Russians (like in '69), or bad race relations (like in '69), or protests on campuses (like in '69). It seems we have lost that spark, just a bit, and that's okay for people like me who had that time, had that foundation of combining dreams with plans, ambitions with determination, like NASA did when I was young. But I wonder what the nine-year-olds today turn to for that lesson of hope, that example of integrity and focus. What field do children's fathers bring them to just before sundown to sit on lawn chairs and wait for what happens? An empty field has the potential of the sum of all possibility.

Humanity needs something larger than itself to shoot for. We can over-focus on tragedies and deceptions, leaving us the impression that today's headlines are the beginning and ending of our existence. In the midst of such madness, striving toward an almost impossible ambition provides the perspective necessary to keep moving forward, to keep hope, to keep enough integrity to recognize we can do better than this. The greatest minds combined in the history of humanity have not yet figured it all out; but the pursuit itself has always been their purpose. We have focused too close to home, aiming merely to achieve; what a disappointing ambition. Perhaps we don't spend enough time outside, where all desire begins, where all hope is born.

Maybe too many people think everything's already been discovered. I'm sure others felt like that every step of the way from the Dark Ages through the Renaissance. Can we reach the stars someday? Hell, I can't even name the damn things, but I'm glad someone smarter than me is mapping the way. It was U.S. astronomer and pioneer of Dark Matter, Vera Rubin, who noted that more than anything else, the discovery of the far reaches of space should teach us humility. We all could use a little reminder that we are at best merely guests here, moving through, making room for others hundreds of years from now to look up at the skies and marvel at the nebula, be amazed again at the craters on the moon.

The Wilderness, Quietly

In Isak Dinesen's story "Wings," she and Denys Finch-Hatton come upon a dead giraffe, shot and abandoned by poachers. Two lions are feeding upon the carcass, and they're the same two which have been terrorizing villagers, so Dinesen and Finch-Hatton decide to go out one night and kill the lions. They do. It's tight writing and exciting narrative with just enough philosophical digression to make the piece not solely about 1920 Kenya.

In the story, Denys points out that the lions were just doing what lions do, and he says they must simply be part of it, quietly. To which Karen Blixen (Dinesen's real name) replies, "And we are just doing what we do. Shoot them."

I would like to blend in to the wilderness more, go unnoticed as Finch-Hatton desired. Some deer will stand still while I walk by, ready to run, determined to stay. Dogs, cats, and even squirrels seem attracted to me, and hummingbirds have taken to zeroing in on my bloodshot eyes. But I'd like to rest along the river or at a pond while wildlife calmly go about their business. I like to observe, to note how they handle the passing of time. I like to watch the osprey glide then find their way to their nest to feed their young. It would be a pleasure to do this without them wanting to fly away. It has certainly made me more stealth.

Still, I believe I'd be more like Karen than Denys. The

man had nerves of steel, but Karen, while nervous, even scared, nonetheless enjoyed the adrenaline rush that often accompanies life. Some endeavors come at a cost, but that cost—which at the extreme can be called a death wish—is what Blixen was doing out there to begin with. I think she just wanted to experience the very happening of life, not its passing.

It is one thing to understand we are alive, here, now, resting on the passing of time. It is an entirely separate situation to be in tune to the pulse of life, to watch its chest rise and fall, to feel the breath of life on the back of your neck. To a certain degree I find that in nature, in my version of wilderness, which seems to be rapidly retreating from the suburbs which have spread out like a flair on a paper towel. In nature, every single time that deer do not move as I walk by is a surprise. Each osprey that dives for a fish and carries it to its young in the nest is nothing short of miraculous. And so too the Carolina wrens when they sing; and the goldfinches, or the indigo buntings.

It has become difficult to be somewhere unarguable, somewhere absent of shallow conflicts, questionable motives. We live our lives in such diluted waters it is hard to tell anymore exactly whose life it is we are living to begin with. Our own? Our spouses? Our parents?

No one's?

When asked by Dinesen why he wouldn't do what she wanted him to do, Finch-Hatton said, plainly, "I don't want to find myself one day at the end of *someone else's* life."

I'll take the wilderness, quietly.

Come 'Round Right

The concept, "If you don't have anything nice to say, don't say anything at all," which I grew up with, is gone. On the news, in the classroom, and even in seemingly innocent conversations, more often than not, people complain.

I'm on a mission to dial back the news to a need-to-know-only basis. It is essential to be well informed, but it is equally essential to be able to separate the news from the noise. My stress level has adjusted up to some higher level of anxiety not at all compensated for by valuable information. Material gathered should be worth the anguish to obtain it. But that simply isn't the case any longer. Now it is just static which causes stress, which doesn't benefit me at all.

Excuse me while I step aside. It won't bother anybody if I simply duck away for a while. Don't pay any mind to me if I move out of the way to let pass the convoy of criticism and manipulation.

I'll just sit and watch the water and wildlife do their thing, the perpetual movement of the tide, the endless flight of thought. My health, my energy, and my stress level are all improved by the absence of the nightly news, which I once revered. And I'm better off without the one-on-one conversations with way too many negative people. I am more likely to live longer, less likely to have a negative disposition, and infinitely more likely to relax by turning away from the nonsense. When I'm at the river and the sun is just changing tones behind clouds in the west, it doesn't make a bit of difference who the president is, what the commentators had to say, which tweets came from which unfocused minds, and what happens next. I am far less interested in who said what than I am in keeping my blood pressure in double digits and my heart rate closer to my age than my golf score.

When the eagle glides from the treetops, and the osprey teach their young to fly, and the clouds at dusk separate colors in prism-like perfection, it is hard to remember what the complaining was all about anyway. We carry our baggage way longer than we ever need to, if we ever really needed to at all. And the answers we seek in day-to-day life won't be unearthed during some pointless pursuit of fair and balanced. Even if I listened more intently to all the facts and expert opinions and came to the correct conclusions agreed upon by Nobel laureates and Pulitzer Prize winning journalists, what then? Then I might know the truth about A and the lies told by B and the injustice we see served to those in need. And then what?

When all I hear is the call of an osprey or the way the waves lap at the edge of the land, I could be in so many other places and so many other times. It is innocent, even ignorant some might say. We live in the age of information, the age of blame, the age of instantaneous and simultaneous where the comment you posted ten minutes ago is now ancient news five screens in the past. It is the age of convenience and the age of emotion and the age of attention-getting-self-indulgent-everyone's opinion matters and is valid and is equal and should be heard. And that's just not true, it is wrong, it is defeatist, and it is destructive.

In nature I have no hoops to jump through. In nature I can come 'round right and simplify my life. My theory is this: I will be healthier, happier, more efficient, more useful and focused, and infinitely more at peace.

I love the way the water feels cool on the soles of my feet on a hot afternoon, or how the salt water gets on my lips and seems to stay there all day, even after I shower. It is as if the movement of the waves exactly coincides with the movement of my blood, and that rhythm somehow settles my soul.

As nature intended.

Flaws

Sometimes I like to make left turns and doing so means adjusting various aspects of life. We can be driven to pursue greater work ambitions for which others may measure our contribution. Other times life grabs us by the collar and says it is time to climb out of the competitive path and onto another, less-traveled one. Time to take Emerson's advice and adopt the pace of nature and understand that her secret is patience.

Our life is a mere odyssey, pilgrimage, journey, with trials and tribulations along the way. It is like we are characters in the story written by someone greater than us. And do we ever have some character flaws. From Odysseus to Don Quixote to Santiago of *Old Man and the Sea* and Allie Fox of *The Mosquito Coast*, pride seems to dominate, some vanity, a little bit of delusion. Maybe I'm too much like Santiago with all of his persistence and stubbornness, but mostly I bend toward Cervantes' most famous character. I don't mind tilting at windmills. I have no problem with self-deception. I know someday someone's going to hold up a mirror so I can see those character flaws, but so far the quixotic ways of life have worked for me. I think my most recent dynamic moment came when I realized sometimes we establish one comfortable way of existence only to learn it is time for what's next.

Are there two paths in the woods from which we can be

only one traveler? Anyone who has spent time here knows there's only one way forward; the proverbial diversion is an illusion. We just need to climb on the donkey and work our way up whatever new hillside we come across.

Still, a walk in the woods can be boring when the path is clear. It is certainly safer to know what obstacles await, but then what is the point of continuing? "Discovery" is the most overlooked character trait of the ordinary soul. Out here in the wilderness it can be just as stressful knowing what's going to happen down the road as it is not knowing at all.

History is riddled with examples of left turns and roundabouts we never anticipated but later can't fathom life without. Richard Jones was working with tension springs when one of them fell to the ground–the slinky. George Crum was a chef in Saratoga Springs who got pissed off when a customer kept sending back her potatoes because they weren't done enough, so he cut them thin and fried them to a crisp. She loved them, he made them a menu item, and potato chips were born. Of course, the Kellogg brothers left a pot of grain boiling on the stove for way too long and the dried mess became corn flakes. George Halas played outfield for the Yankees but hurt his hip. He was replaced by two new players–Sammy Vick and Babe Ruth. Halas' injury made it possible for Ruth to get game time every day, but it also enabled Halas to move to Chicago and become one of the greatest football coaches of all time.

You never know. But it invokes the scary question: just how far down the road do you really want to see? I'm not suggesting a complete abandonment of one way of life for the unknown of another. I just think stepping aside for a moment in this brief pilgrimage through life to understand that in the end we will have to answer to ourselves, is worth such a brief pause.

Abandoning life as we know it for life as it can be is not "quitting," and it is not "giving up." No. As Rousseau relates: "Has it ever been said that a man who throws himself out the window to escape from a fire is guilty of suicide?"

Wildly Unpredictable

Fall has arrived and the breezes this weekend cleared away most of what was left of summer. Last week I walked along the river like I always do, and this time of year when the water laps at my feet, it is warmer than the air, inviting, deceiving, teasing me into thinking summer will push back on autumn and maybe even win out. I don't mind the change so much; I'm not bothered by the passing of time as much as how I *spend* the passing of time.

Sometimes you can see all the changes happen in one day. Crazy.

The truth is some things need to change. Even with resistance, sometimes it is the only way to make room for new growth. For me even the seasonal change from summer to fall is often troublesome. Again, I don't mind fall—my days in northern states are most memorable for this time of year. And obviously I know it is going to happen. I watch the weather, I mark the calendar, I see the leaves letting go. But still it always takes me by surprise. I wake up one day and I need to wear more clothes, or I no longer feel the sun so strong on my shoulders, and I am saddened. I spend nearly all my time in nature, and still it startles me when things change.

When a change is even more unexpected than in nature, like anyone else I wonder how I am going to handle it. And the surest way—for me anyway—to gauge my reaction to life being different or accepting some sort of radical, unexpected shift in existence is to look back to when these things have happened before.

In kindergarten I liked a little red-haired girl, Kathleen. Just like Charlie Brown, I was afraid to approach her. We were in the same class until third grade when at the end of the school year my family moved away. Instead of saying goodbye to her I made a card that said, "I love you" and threw it at her in the hallway. I think she got it. Now I wish I had just handed it to her politely and said I was sorry I was moving. I never saw her again. I probably didn't handle that relationship well.

In some ways that's all of us in our youth. I often ignored advice of my older siblings, examples set down on television or in school. I simply preferred to assess a situation and have at it on my own terms, even if it meant complete and utter disaster. Once I walked three blocks from home just to play with a friend's plastic bowling pin set. I was eight. Another time I decided to hike into the San Jacinto Mountains outside Palm Springs without telling my parents, or anyone for that matter. I missed the small sign that said "Danger: Rattle Snake Area. Keep Out." What a beautiful hike that was until I fell into a Saguaro cactus and spent an extra hour on a rock pulling thorns out of my leg. What a great day. Nature takes us into the unknown, of course, but it gives us such satisfaction when doing so. Imagine that for a second. No satellite photos, no GPS, no maps and indicators, no sextant, nothing but perhaps some paths beaten by cattle or floods. Wild. Roethke reminds us that over every mountain is a path, though it may not be seen from the valley.

Still, I should be dead from venom poisoning. Or abducted. Or in juvi for harassing an eight-year-old girl. Instead, I gained the confidence we used to earn on our own, trying and failing, fantasizing and acting and pretending. You simply never know when those youthful lessons will come in handy, see us through an unexpected left-turn, help us through the changes. I thought about those years, my early youth and how innocent it all was; how we flipped baseball cards and played stickball. We had block parties where the block would be closed to traffic and we all put picnic tables and grills out and walked up and down the street talking to everyone else and sharing food, and riding bikes, and the adults had drinks and the kids had fun. Television went off the air at night, just a fuzzy white noise until the early morning when a black-and-white flag waved across the screen and some dude said, "We now begin our broadcast day" after the National Anthem.

This was the age of my youth. It was innocent and tech-free and filled with hippies and protests and flag-burning and marches and sit-ins and rumbles. The laughable Mets became the champs and we walked on the moon. On the moon, for God's sake. How can you possibly not understand why at the core of my generation is some semblance of hope still simmering? We were not a generation of followers staring at our hands; not by any stretch of the imagination. When the times were a 'changing, we changed—or we were the ones causing the change to begin with. And as we grew older, those organic traits became part of our DNA.

Change is part of who we are and is absolutely dependent upon how we were when we were young. And when I was young I was restless, always ready for something new. I didn't mind our move away from the little red-haired girl. I didn't mind the move to Virginia.

I welcome what's next. Maybe that's why the pathless wood doesn't scare me as much as highway signs and road maps.

Migration

The water in the Chesapeake when the tide rises and fills the Rappahannock will have an identity crisis as it moves past the mouth of the river and floods the marsh at the end of my road messing with the salinity. Still, it adapts. The water moves and swirls and ebbs and floods; it finds new ways to cut crevices in sand and even rock. And the water which runs past my calves on a warm May afternoon might have once cut its way through limestone up river near Luray and will slap against a fishing boat out beyond the continental shelf towards Bermuda.

"I am haunted by water," wrote Norman MacLean. So am I.

The earth is 71 percent water. Babies are born about 78 percent water, and that drops to about 60 percent by adulthood. Of all the water in the world, only about 2.5 percent of it is fresh. And 68 percent of the fresh water is found in inaccessible ice caps and glaciers. If you're out looking for any though, the best place to fill your canteen is Lake Baikal in Siberia, which contains about 20 percent of the world's fresh water (the unfrozen non-glacier type, except in winter). That's changing, obviously. In fact, right now only about 30 percent of fresh water can be found in the ground. This means of all the water in the world, only a small fraction is drinkable.

I dehydrate very easily so I am always drinking my share, and probably your share. I like water. It energizes me. I can do that. But about 1.5 million children die every year because of lack of water or having access to only low-quality water. The thing is, water is life. Even when searching for life on other planets, it is actually water they are looking for. At the same time, water kills. My brother lives southeast of Houston, Texas, and through some combination of miracle and excellent planning on his part he was not flooded by the rising waters associated with hurricanes. But too many people to count lost their homes, lost their lives. It isn't hard to understand why floods are the primary weather-related cause of death in the world.

My son and I hired a car and driver along with a translator in Irkutsk and headed north out of the city to the villages along Lake Baikal. It was a foggy day, the air wet but warm enough, and we walked to a dock where an older man was getting in a small boat to fish. He stood next to us describing the waters, the countless tributaries coming into the lake from the frozen north, but only one river out, the Angara, which heads south into Mongolia. Then he leaned over and told us when the water is still as it was that day, you can see a dozen meters deep, and it isn't unusual to see seals swimming by below.

We were surrounded by water; clear, deep, pure fresh water and we were as far from western civilization as you can get. GPS doesn't work there. Cell phones are pointless. We stepped over the edge. World history there has more blank spaces than perhaps anywhere else on the planet. For many of the residents in some remote sections of Siberia,

Columbus never set sail, the Wright Brothers never took off, and Neil Armstrong is a myth. I understand why the czars in St. Petersburg and leaders in Moscow considered exile there to be punishment enough. It simply doesn't exist unless you are already there. To the rest of the world, the landscape is a mystery and the people are all ghosts. And we are not so much travelers as we are brief shadows in the land of the midnight sun.

But a few weeks later we arrived in Vladivostok on the Sea of Japan where we were cautioned against drinking tap water. The Fukushima nuclear disaster, caused by an earthquake and tsunami, had occurred just two years earlier, and there was some concern the contaminated deluge might still be swirling through the Pacific. I drank beer instead.

And when we returned I made my normal, post-remote-world visit to the doctor and cardiologist, who said I needed to keep my blood pressure down, so he prescribed a diuretic to reduce the fluid in my body.

Yes, I am haunted by water. And through all my travels, water has been my salvation, my remedy, my enemy, my life. Which is why whenever I arrive home, I keep moving, walking the far reaches of the marshes along the bay and river. Here, nearly every evening in winter just before dusk bends to night, in those moments after twilight when I let my eyes adjust to the lack of light, a few hundred geese land in the pond, some on the river, and a few in the field nearby.

I can hear them for quite some time before they actually fly into sight from beyond the trees to the west. The air is so clear this time of year I can hear them honking in groups, joining in like a chorus which starts with just a few voices and adds another rafter until they reach some crescendo.

At first it might be only a flight of a dozen or so based upon the muted sound from the distance. But over the course of five minutes or ten I hear another group, then another, and more. They fly in a "V" to be able to see each other clearly for protection and create just a little draft, but the closer they come to landing, the faster the formation falls apart.

Eventually the first group is already in the pond when the last group crests the bare branches of the oaks, and hundreds settle into the field or onto the river. One time thousands landed on the plowed cornfield just down river. Their honking continued for an hour that night, and just as the sounds of these geese slowly softens and, finally, quiets, so did theirs so that from my porch I could tell they had all landed safely.

But every single time long after the large group arrives, two or three geese come in late, alone, as if they stopped at another farm over near the bay and had to regroup and find their flock.

I don't want to disturb them, but I always want to watch. So when I walk along the river at that hour and the skin on my face is tight from the cold, and my nose runs a little, and the muscles in my back are also tight from the cold, I keep my hands thrust into the pockets of my coat and walk along the soft shoulder of the tiny dead end road so that my feet make no noise. I can usually get to the narrow strip of sand at the river from where I can see both it and the pond, but not the field so well. Their call increases in a burst of warnings to the rest that I'm around. It quiets quickly though as I remain still and sit on the cold rip rap running along the river and blend into the rocks and am no longer a threat.

On winter nights the water is almost always calm, a

slow methodic lap at the rocks and sand. The sky is all stars, and sometimes just after dark in January you can still find the center of the Milky Way in the southwest. With no unnatural lights for more than twenty miles in any direction except from the scattered farmhouses or buoys, the sky is a carpet of constellations.

It isn't by chance my Canada friends find respite here. They need grass for food, they need water, and they need to be able to see great distances to anticipate danger. That's why they're here on the edge of the bay with open fields and ponds. It also explains why they love airports and golf courses. The abundance of geese isn't an accident either; they travel in gangs, often the younger geese are forced into the gang, so that traveling is safe, and they can better dominate such areas.

But their coolest trait is their honk. They keep that up as a form of encouragement so the lead geese will maintain their speed and not give out so easily. Basically, the ones in the back are telling the ones up front to "Go! Go! Go! Go!" and move their asses. And when the lead gets tired, she moves to the back and gets to badger the others for a while. And they do this their whole lives—about twenty-seven years.

And just after twilight when dusk is making its brief appearance, and the water is like a mirror, the call of the geese from well across the treetops is musical, somehow eternal. When this land was unbroken, Canada geese called to each other, rushing for the open fields and waterways, settling down here. Powhatan heard geese here, and John Smith, and Washington just to the north at his birthplace on the Potomac, and Jefferson not far from there. Through the centuries the flyway from the St. Lawrence down across the Adirondacks and Catskills to the Susquehanna south into Virginia to the mouths of these five fair rivers spilling into the Chesapeake has been their home.

And they love dusk, just before dark, as it is the best time of day for them to recalibrate their internal magnetic compass to cross continents; to come here year after year.

We have that in common: we're both very migratory; we both end up here. I guess that's what also attracts me to the passing flocks of geese. The peace in such sounds late on a winter's evening touches my soul, settles me somehow beyond my ability to explain. But also, I sit on the rip rap and blend into the rocks and watch them in the water and contemplate their distance from the central regions of Ontario and Quebec, across Hudson Bay. My entire life I've been drawn to migration, to some sense of movement from one place to another, particularly the seeming randomness of such order. They know where they are going every time, and yet they move south without boundaries, schedules, or maps. I envy them that, to be always in this retreat, this third place, which for them is work, home, and salvation.

When I was young my father bought me Robin Lee Graham's *Dove*. It was the first book I remember inciting in me a sense of adventure, travel and exploration. The sea seemed to have no borders or barriers. Graham's goal was circumnavigation, but his schedule was wide open. Peter Jenkins, too, in his *A Walk Across America*, knew where he would end up, he just didn't know when or how; and along the way the adventure was in the places he paused for food and water, with an open view of life around him. Ironically, I like the consistency of this migration; the predictable return, surrounded by friends, a quiet night.

I suppose all dreams are migratory, both in hopeful destinations and their transience with the changes in our responsibilities and circumstances. At times I take flight, abandon my flock and push off for a while. But I look forward to coming home to settle into some sense of domesticity, which I can accommodate briefly at best, because eventually I think about the dreams of my youth as I fly toward my twilight years. They call to me to "Go Go Go Go" as my life moves further along, pushing at the edges of dusk.

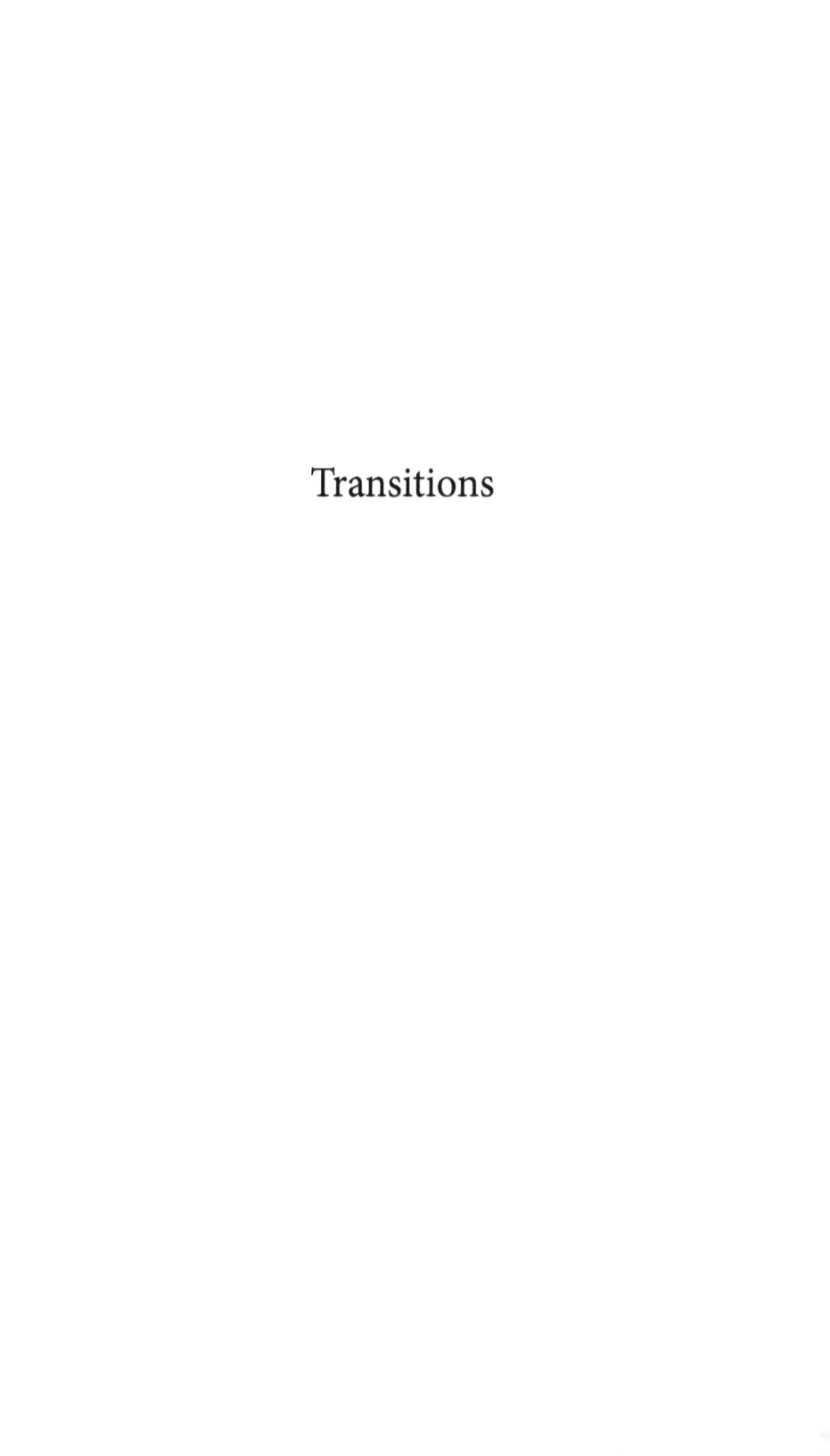

Transitions

Break Away

My high school prom theme was "Breakaway" by Art Gar-funkel. I remember a lot of friends found it cynical, and maybe a bit uncool for the times. We had just snuck past disco and Manilow, so we were really hoping for something edgy, but we ended up with a non-Simon Garfunkel. In fact, I might have been the only one who couldn't get the song out of my head, not in a "tune won't go away" fashion, but the sentiment. It captured exactly what I was feeling at the time.

I watch the distant lights on the runway, Disappear into the evening sky

Any song or poem or movie or work of art or conversation which steered toward distant places and beyond the horizon instantly attached themselves to my psyche. Even then I could feel time like drips of water on the back of my neck.

It's not the sun you're trying to find; Something else is on your mind.

You need a little space and time to break away

I love those lines.

I took a gap year. It wasn't called a gap year back then; it was called the not-go-to-college-and-be-lazy-for-a-year year. I just figured sometime during those twelve months before I headed to the hills of western New York for college, something amazing would fall in my lap. I kept thinking if I kept looking around I'd find something that would have changed everything. I looked around but nothing changed.

You ever feel like you're just one thought away from exactly what you want to say? That was what that whole year felt like; like I was onto something but couldn't quite put my finger on it. A year passed and one of my friends headed to Nashville, another pursued local media, another married and had a child, another started sliding away. I left.

Break away, fly across your ocean. Break away, time has come for you.

Break away, fly across your ocean. Break away, time has come . . .

New York. Arizona. Mexico. New England. Pennsylvania. Virginia. A bunch of foreign lands.

. . . and I'm back. Got a job teaching at the local college none of us ever wanted to attend to begin with. I broke away several dozen times through the years to places all over the world, but I kept coming back. Turns out there were a few things from high school I'm glad I left behind, a few I wish I had never abandoned, and one or two I'm glad I took with me, the most important being that sense of standing on that edge, the sense of leaning forward and jumping off, the sense of possibility and hope.

When I returned all those years later all those years ago, I discovered I wasn't like any of the people I knew in high school save one—the only other one to leave the area. It isn't the "leaving" that connects us, or even the coming back; it is the idea that we are still trying to break away from complacency, from predictability and lack of passion. I still don't feel like I've done it, so I keep thinking it is time for me . . .

To awaken in another country. Greet the morning under foreign skies

And then it hit me. It is the "looking" that I was after. It was the pursuit of what's next that I wanted to pursue, not some place or event or career—but the actual act of simply looking around, as if somewhere back in 1960 God said, "I'm just going to drop you off here for a while so you can check everything out," and simply not sitting around would be my measure of success.

This morning I was on the pier at the oceanfront. It was foggy and I couldn't see beyond the surf break. I stared at the fog for quite some time, the mist, and how it beautifully shrouded the fishermen on the pier, the scattered tourists on the beach, the sculptures up and down the boardwalk. I watched a young boy try and bait his hook, and I talked to an old man about how the selection of fish has changed through the decades. I watched a lone surfer let lesser waves roll by. At some point I thought about what it was like a bit further out to sea. It was brighter beyond the fog and I knew that out on the horizon the sun was inevitably pushing through, we just couldn't see it. I turned and watched walkers and joggers pause at the rail waiting for the sun to come through and I turned back and had this overwhelming desire to borrow the man's surfboard and push out beyond the fog and go looking for the sun. I thought how cool it must be for the fishing boats already out past the shelf searching the deep waters to be able to feel the sun on their faces, pulling in their catch while gulls dive nearby, while back on shore people wait for that morning light to come to them.

And, of course, like some trite metaphor just waiting to pounce, I stood at the end of the pier and realized:

It's not the sun I'm trying to find, it's something else that's on my mind.

I just need a little space and time to break away.

The Value of Change

When I was a child I found an oak near the creek at the end of the old trail along the Southern State Parkway, and I carved my name in the trunk. It might still be there, nearly half a century later; if some hurricane hasn't taken it down, or some summer storm, or construction or a myriad other ways time steals our past.

This weekend while out walking along the Rappahannock River in Virginia I wondered if I decided to drive to the very end of that Long Island road and park near our old house and walk through the woods to the trail, would I discover fourteen-year-old me standing there with a knife not understanding how fast the tree would widen and distort my name? Would I stare across decades and measure the distance from my youth by the height and breadth of the trees I long ago climbed and swung from and hid behind? Nothing exceptional happened in those woods; nothing but the passing of time occurred where I carved my name in a tree while Dad waited at home for us to move on. But when I returned to my car would I catch a glimpse of my long-ago father looking at the newly planted trees surrounding our new house anticipating their eventual majesty? Did we know we would move away so soon? Do we ever know how soon we move away?

So many seasons have passed, and once again leaves are

ablaze, burnt orange and fire-red. It is as if new colors appear, and my son has spent his own decades taking pictures and marking time by the height of the apple trees in our yard, which anyway have lost their leaves for now. Everywhere I look it is autumn and the branches more prominent, like bones pushing through aged skin. If my father were still here would he want to tell me again about the colors on the trees along the Brooklyn streets of his youth? I have never been able to take root like him, but I've come to understand the arch of ancestry and the unwavering value of the past.

And what value there is in every moment, in every season. What profound and inexplicable value exists in the persistent passing of time, the predictability of change, and the colors of life. Oh! Such colors of life!

Serendip Revisited

One night in Norway about three a.m. I had to pee and the only place was an outhouse fifty feet behind the cabin. It was negative something and knee-deep snow, but I got dressed and headed out. I had to wait, though, because at the same time my colleague Joe had the same idea and was already in there. After we both did our thing, we were wide awake so we decided to hike up a snowy service road next to the house. That night we saw moose, more stars than I knew existed, and green bands of the aurora borealis bouncing around the sky like a wind-blown towel.

Vincent van Gogh once went for a walk and came home and wrote his brother Theo this:

The earth has been thought to be flat. It was true, and is today, that between Paris and Arles, it is. But science has proven the world is round and nobody contradicts that nowadays. But notwithstanding all of this people persist in believing that life is flat and runs from birth to death. However, life too is probably round, and very superior in expanse and capacity to the hemisphere we know at present. For my part I know nothing of it. I feel more and more that we must not judge God on the basis of this world; it is a study that didn't come off. What can you do in a study that has gone wrong if you are fond of the artist? You do not find much to criticize; you hold your tongue. But you have a right to ask for something better. It is only a master than can make such a muddle as this, since then we have a right to see the same creative hand get even with itself. And this life of ours, so much criticized and for such good and exalted reasons—we must not take it for anything more than it is and go on hoping that in some other life we'll see a better thing than this.

Depressing no doubt, and probably written on his down cycle of mania, but beautiful nonetheless. At first, I dug into van Gogh's life because I was fascinated by the reality that while alive he was considered not simply a failure, but an embarrassment in the art world, and yet he went on to become one of the most influential artists in history. Not everything is as it seems; not everyone is of the same mold.

Van Gogh is a lesson in passion and confidence, in pursuing one's objective despite criticism and dissent. This isn't to suggest we run blindly into a pathless wood; but there is value in internal motivation. Van Gogh only wrote letters because he wanted to tell his brother where the money loaned to him was being spent, and while explaining he digressed into philosophy. He only decided to become a painter because he got kicked out of the church where he wanted to be a preacher, fired from his uncle's art dealership because he didn't like the patrons' tastes in art, and kicked out of the academy for disagreeing with the teachers. He only decided to paint because he was too much of a bastard to do anything else.

Naturally this made me think of Horace Walpole.

He was the 4th Earl of Oxford and a man of letters who read Persian fairytales in the 1700s. In his work, "The Three Princes of Serendip," the heroes consistently make fascinating discoveries while searching for something else on a small island with the Arabic name of Sarandip, later

Serendip, known now as Sri Lanka. Walpole coined the word "serendipity" to reference someone who makes a discovery while looking for something else, or in many cases, finding perfection while not looking for anything at all.

We all go looking for one thing and often find something else. It turns out the greatest proof of absolute symmetry in life is the complete randomness of it all. Alexander Fleming sneezed in a Petri dish full of bacteria and discovered penicillin. His famous quote followed: "Nature made penicillin, I just found it. One sometimes finds what one is not looking for."

What's ironic is it isn't always the spectacular events which redirect the flow of our existence; it is the small curves which surprise us into new landscapes. Life bends and twists and folds back on itself. "You never know" might just be one of the greatest truisms of all time.

The Call of the Foghorns

The geese are back. They fly over my house every night in winter. From late afternoon until after midnight flocks of geese pass or land or take off from the wealth of local waterways. Some settle in small ponds, but most gather in the harvested fields. Usually they commute in groups of fifteen or twenty, but I've heard their honking and stepped onto the porch to see upwards of two hundred fly by. One time they were so loud in the field I went out to find thousands of geese settling in before continuing to who knows where. Their stay is swift, albeit perennial.

And last week in the dead of Spring they uncharacteristically crossed the twilight sky. It is that sound, though, the whoosh of wings in a methodical push along with their familiar call, which remains as true and consistent in my life as the sounds of birds in the morning. Here along the bay some geese nest all year, but it is in winter when migration routes from the St. Lawrence Seaway to all points south steer them into the area after dusk. I have laid in bed well into the evening and listened to them move past in the cold, clear sky. Sometimes I sit on the porch expecting, hoping, knowing they'll be back.

But the migration of geese in and of itself is not what keeps my attention in this narrative, even in June when they're more abundant in January. It is their sound and the way it always calls to me, like so many sounds in our lives. Nature does nothing in vain, Aristotle said.

When I was young the foghorns in the early hours called out from the boats on the Great South Bay. I remember waking to their long, singular tone warning other fishing vessels headed out or coming in across the reach. Foghorns will always remind me of my adolescence and riding bikes out on early spring weekend mornings with my friends, a band of twelve-year-olds biking it to the bay through the fog and up to the docks. On clear days we could see Fire Island, but some mornings we couldn't even see each other, and being that close to the water so early meant feeling the booming vibrations from foghorns. I can still smell the marsh on the nearby river and feel the cool wetness of the salty air on my skin.

And I know as long as I find my way to the water in winter I can count on the geese overhead, calling across the river. If I was to head back to the Island and one night went to the docks at Timber Point, I am certain I'd not recognize the area for how much has changed. There might be more traffic nearby, and the number of leisure boats has most likely increased. But all these decades later I am equally certain the sound of foghorns would drift toward shore in the morning as certain as a flock of geese migrate through these local fields, even now on the front edge of summer.

Twenty years ago I built this house in the wilderness, frequented by hawks, the occasional eagle, countless osprey, and on winter evenings, geese. In recent years the number of bald eagles has increased. I have never been complacent watching such majestic birds of prey in flight. One move of her wings and an eagle can glide on a draft clear across the river before turning east across the bay. Still, they make no sounds. Oh, sometimes hawks call out to each other in a very distinct high pitch caw. But mostly they perch in silence. Their lack of sound creates a distance between us like strangers in a waiting room. Once I walked back from the river and saw an adult bald eagle atop the house. But because of the raptor's silence and blank stare, we lacked connection, some sort of shared space.

Despite my own random migrations, I find comfort in the familiar. The sounds of those I have loved and lost talk to me sometimes when I sit at night on the porch and recall long-ago conversations. We can be haunted by sound.

In a world where we often seek silence to escape the noise, it is the laughter of friends and companions that calls to us through the fog of daily life and steers us home. Pavlov wasn't far off, but the bells which I respond to are the sounds of friends laughing, family telling stories, a football game on television on Thanksgiving Day with the smell of turkey filling the house, an old western on a rainy summer Saturday afternoon. I love the daily calls of life, the drifting sounds on a summer evening, the persistence of the ocean waves, the relentless ranting of house wrens in the morning.

Wine glasses. Dice on a game board in the other room. The quiet wisp of golf on television. Steaks on a hot grill. Bacon in a pan in the morning. New friends drinking wine, laughing. Children.

There But For

Mother Theresa. Malcolm X. Neil Armstrong. Jimi Hendrix. Pope Paul the Sixth. Lech Walesa. St. John Paul the Second. Thomas Merton. President General Eisenhower. Elvis. Pablo Picasso. Albert Schweitzer.

Rwandan Tutsis. The Lost Boys of Sudan. Steven Biko. Pol Pot.

I shared time with these people; I stood witness to their events. These saints and sinners brushed my sleeve simply by sharing the earth during my stay. We have a loose connection to miracles and massacres.

An old dilapidated house near my home dates to the 1700s. It sits in the middle of what was once a slave plantation. Just across the land long ago gone were the slave quarters. Today the house is covered by vines and trees; some dying themselves after a century of life. Generations of neighbors have come and gone, and generations of foliage and storms and crops have come and gone and what's left of the house crumbles into the earth.

Some say let it crumble; some say tear it down and build a new place on the land and give it to the slaves' descendants, many of whom still live on the same road; oppressed people either stay close to home or they never come back.

When I walk past I am painfully aware that I shared this space, separated only by time, with people who whipped men and women, others who were whipped and shackled. This isn't a movie; it isn't even history when you stand on the muddy lane at the end of the path and look toward the once-was porch and picture a fine-dressed overseer ordering humans to commit inhumane acts. This is where I live. We live. My friends freezing up in Buffalo and my family on the Gulf Coast all live here too; just beyond reach, a little out of time.

This world has some serious issues; always has. It is at best, though, a hotel, and every once in a while I take a look at the register to remind myself who else stayed here. Alexander the Great, Charlemagne, Mohammed, Ivan the Terrible, Ghengis Khan, all guests just over the slope of the horizon, just beyond some small slice of linear time. On the same human trajectory as mine but before, is Geronimo, Moses, Jesus, think about the gentle bend of time, the careen of place that separates me from the disciples, the Visigoths, the founding fathers. All here but just before.

Closer to now, when I look inside the lines of my coming and going, between those two rays shooting off from my birth and my death, I can see the souls who at one time or another shared with me this spinning blue wad. Not short of miraculous, we claim the same particles of stardust, and that's what keeps me looking around when I walk down some city street; I want to know who else is on earth with me.

My swift life falls on the same graph as Richard Wright and Ernest Hemingway. And when that shack in the woods around the corner from my home was still in its prime, the walls still absorbing the shrieks of rape, the cries of bleeding men, Grandma Moses was a toddler. Grandma Moses, who painted her last work about the time I learned to swim. I was alive when someone was alive who was alive during the Civil War.

Carl Jung lectured during my youth, and Ty Cobb watched the same Mets players as me. When I was still cutting new teeth and outgrowing my Keds, I could have headed downtown with my Dad and possibly been on the same train as William Faulkner, ee cummings or Marilyn Monroe. I might have passed them on the street, maybe stood in line at some drug store counter with my mom and behind us because of the blending of circumstance might have been Sylvia Plath or Sam Cooke; Nat King Cole; Otis Redding. We have overlapping lives. On a circle graph, we share the shaded space.

Judy Garland and I watched the New York Jets in Super Bowl Three. When I was born World War One vets weren't yet senior citizens and World War Two vets were in their thirties. Vietnam isn't history to me; it is my childhood, my early teens. The fall of Saigon was announced over the loud speakers at my high school.

There are empty fields save monuments and markers where soldiers died defending this land against the British, against ourselves, and they stood where I stand and watched the hazy sun rise. Same sun; same beach, same blessed Commonwealth. Don't mistake history for "back then." Those people just happened to check out before us. It could have been us. It is us now. And it won't be long before our lives overlap with the crying call of a newborn Einstein. Did you see that boy running at the park? That girl climbing the tree at her home? Did I just pass by some senator, some Cicero or Socrates, some St Augustine?

Like strangers buying the same house decades before,

like seeing the list of who owned the used car, like getting a job replacing some retiree. Like standing in line. Like sourdough starter. Like a relay race.

I like knowing the people I know now, these brothers and sisters, whose overlapping lives linger just within my time frame; we share the same air, watch the same news and celebrate the same wins. In some divine book somewhere, these people and I are on the same page. My parents, my siblings, my children, my God what grace to have shared this passage from cradle to grave.

Six Months After My Father's Death

(with apologies to Albert Einstein)

How long is six months? Well, obviously, logically speaking it is simple math: 182 days, or 4368 hours. I can prove this; I counted. But it is not how I perceive six months. When a child moves from one year to eighteen months old, we are excited by the new date: "He is eighteen months old today!" we exclaim to questioning gawkers. But at fifty-five I didn't say, "Well, actually I'm fifty-five and a half today."

Six months means so much more on the edges of life than it does in the middle.

When I am entirely in the moment–focused and engaged–time is irrelevant. I couldn't tell you if an hour passed or a week. It is only when I think about it that the laws of relativity engage. I would like a life where I remain completely in each moment. My "String Theory" is to have a string of *those* moments, from cradle to grave. But perception is an unfriendly conspirator in linear time.

It was a Wednesday night, about eight-thirty, and I just had finished teaching creative writing. The winter which passed after that Wednesday seemed to be milder than previous years. There were some cold days, and I remember a stretch in January when we needed to let the faucet drip upstairs, but mostly it was fine, the ground never too frozen.

Still, the trees are not much different in April than they were in October, the borders of two seasons, one going and one coming back, separated by mostly bare branches and plowed fields. Even the fairways at the golf course are the same half-brown, half-green as each other; this time the green is on the way in instead of on the way out, and life is returning in the rough.

October and April are first cousins.

Excuse me for this but I "wikied" Time. Here's what it said: "Time is the indefinite continued progression of existence and events that occur in apparently irreversible succession from the past through the present to the future."

Apparently.

As usual, Wikipedia is only partly right. That's a fine explanation of linear time, thank you. But it doesn't account for emotion or recollection. Perception. I learned much about our perception of time simply by spending some with my father. A round of golf, for instance, went much faster when we played well than when we didn't. Watching baseball games on television wasn't unlike being held hostage; they seemed to last so long. But when we showed up at Shea Stadium for a Mets Game, nine innings passed in minutes. And two fingers of Scotch can somehow simultaneously last forever and disappear without notice. It all depends, and that is what's cool about time—it is much less scientific than it appears.

"All our sweetest hours fly fastest," wrote Virgil. No kidding.

I once didn't see someone for twenty-three years and then one day I did, and it was as if no time at all had passed. This morning I spoke to a colleague and I thought I aged a decade just standing there. Perception.

If someone gives up cigarettes or alcohol for six months, it is a major achievement. If someone has a new job for six months he or she is still suspect. And in love: "They only knew each other six months" is diametrically opposed to "You mean you've not spoken for six months?!" But I've spent enough time on rivers to understand there is "no such thing as time," as Hesse points out. "At the mouth, at the waterfall, at the ferry, at the current, in the ocean and in the mountains, everywhere, and the present only exists for it, not the shadow of the past nor the shadow of the future."

Six months isn't always six months. Sometimes measurement is pointless.

The Mets won the National League pennant that night, that Wednesday. Six months later brought the opening month of the baseball season, which, six months from now, will be over and we will have a new World Series champion. The half year to the next World Series seems so much further away than the six months since the last one, or is that just me? It was 76 degrees that day with an evening low of 45. Fall was holding off as long as possible. I taught creative writing that night, finishing about eight-thirty.

A student commented it was too early to end, and I agreed, but I left anyway.

A doctor I know said the passing of time is relative to experience. When we miss someone, it seems so much longer since we have seen him. It is all perception. That's what disappoints about time: as an objective process it is relatively persistent, dependable. Relentless, in fact. I can tell you the definitive truth about how long it will take for six months to pass. But I can't begin to measure what it will feel like.

Why does six months from now seem so much further

away than six months ago? I suppose time recedes quicker than it approaches. Anticipation has a lot to do with that, and regret. They so work against each other. "I wish I could have" implies something happened, still fresh and recent, and we missed the chance to say or do or try something. However, "I can't wait until" implies some event seems like it will never get here.

Maybe time isn't linear after all. We can manipulate time by recalling just the right moment, smelling some fragrance, hearing the right song—they bring us right back, right there. You can't slap that into an equation. Measuring how we experience time means allowing for some x-factor, be it love, or fear, or loss, which renders the numbers pointless. Six months? It was yesterday. It was a lifetime ago.

Step outside and look at the sun. Take five minutes, call your Dad for five minutes while outside looking at the sun.

Really, only five minutes.

Part Two

Well Before Dawn

I am drawn toward the early morning hours of dawn, when I feel ahead of the world, and I can sense some small whisper of . . . what . . . hope, I suppose, or wonder maybe. To hear life around the river in those moments motivates me, awakens in me possibilities which otherwise lie dormant. Before the sun rises, often just after the first sliver of light reaches up across the bay, I can hear osprey and other sea birds who at that hour never seem to mind my presence.

But earlier, when that glimmer on the eastern horizon is still merely a possibility, I have taken to walks by moonlight, sometimes not even that. In the woods where I live and down along the water, something is going on. There is life out there wide awake and moving through the dark hours like spirits who need to finish their errands before the sun gives them up. Like sneaking up on some grand behind-the-scenes operation, or suddenly discovering the dark web and meddling around a bit, those hours when the rest of our lives are at rest, motionless, recharging, the world around us is in full swing on the midnight shift.

Generally, this happens for me just before the wildlife around me packs it in for the day; just before I watch the horizon for illumination.

Foxes come about the edges of the woods looking for scraps of food or the peels and rinds of bananas and melons. I can stand patiently and one fox will wander across the yard from the woods behind me to those on the south and stop before disappearing again beyond the laurel, and he will stare at me, relaxed, nosing around the base of a tree where I occasionally put food. Then he's off—not swiftly or in fear, but nonchalantly, demonstrating that he lives here as well and has decided to stretch his legs. That's all.

Owls, too—some barn but mostly screech owls, perch in the oaks and elms, sometimes swooping down and moving through branches with precision. But my favorite are the geese which cover the night sky in flocks sometimes so enormous the swoosh of their wings alone creates a breeze, and their call to "Go! Go! Go!" is startling.

Closer to home, out front near the edge of the trees, deer nearly always feed on the dew-soaked grass and often the hostas, and if they sense me sitting on the porch or standing in the clearing, they will look up, briefly, ears turned forward—just for a moment—and then return to their grass, not minding me, aware just the same. And it is then, when I am well acclimated with the night and my eyes have adjusted, and my soul too has adjusted, that I think of my own way in the world, the motivation behind the turns and hesitations, my purpose of this passing in time. Oh, do I ever have an internal monologue underway with others gathered in my nocturnal imagination! There's one friend nodding his head and insisting I follow my own path. I can hear him clearly when I'm out there, see his small sardonic smile as he says, "Come on Kunzinger. You know how to do this, stop waiting for approval or it's never going to happen." And there, too, is another friend whose smile is as wide as dawn pressing his sense of adventure into my spirit with an "all or nothing" carelessness about him which brings me up short yet livens my ambition. In one brief moment, I am eased by no longer thinking of them in the past tense. Then, just as quickly, we all move on.

And then the distance across the reach lightens ever so slightly, from dark, almost navy blue to something slightly more pale, like powder, and I'm alone again—the fox rushing off into the woods, the geese at rest in the harvested field or at the river's edge, and the murmurs of chickadees and wrens and cardinals chase away what's left of the stillness, and even my friends bow off, and I have trouble separating memory from imagination.

It's as if time lets me manipulate her however I wish just by heading outside at just the right moment; as if time has been neglected, ignored, or taken for granted, but for some of us who stay up late or get up early to gather as much out of our moments that we can, it offers a small reward, and I can bend her ever so slightly. Then, just briefly, it eases the almost vague pain in my soul which gathers around loss, which surrounds emptiness, and which almost always seems to visit during those late-night hours.

Permanent Change

I know nothing is as permanent as nature, despite the constant changes. It simply isn't going anywhere. We are. A century ago farmers sat here and talked about the bounty in the soil, or talked to 19th century watermen about the changing tides. And I like to realize that a hundred years before that the nearby swampland, now home to so many osprey and egrets, was a major route for runaway slaves. They'd have been safe in these woods, if there were woods then.

I like to do that because it reminds me a hundred years *from now* perhaps I will have left some sort of evidence of my passing through; even if just in the cultivation of language, the farming of words.

I sit on the porch and listen to the wind through the leaves. It is now; it is right here, now. Sometimes at night we stand in the driveway with the telescope and study Saturn or contemplate the craters on the moon—both here long before us and in some comforting way, long after we're gone. In spring and fall the bay breezes bring music even Vivaldi would envy, and I'll listen to his *Four Seasons*, written nearly four hundred years ago, and listen to the wind through the leaves of these majestic, young trees reaching eighty feet high, and be completely, perfectly in the moment.

Despite the warming trends, the extreme tendencies of

weather, the fragile ecosystem which sustains life, nature is still the only place I have found that really doesn't change. It never has. Ice ages and dust bowls will alter it, but eventually some seed will take root.

This land has beautiful eighty-foot oaks, some maples, tall thin pines and various other hardwoods including black walnut trees, which I am told can provide the ingredient necessary in the liqueur, Wild Spiced Nocino. The branches protect birds as diverse as red-tailed hawks, downy woodpeckers, and countless chickadees, and they are habitat to other wildlife including one flying squirrel we spotted a few years ago when his tree fell. The squirrel was fine and found a new home in a white oak. But a hundred years ago this was just land, sandy land, edged by the running Rappahannock River and backed by equally treeless farmland. A century before that these nearby plantations provided food for the region at the expense of slavery, and some slave descendants remain, selling vegetables at food carts out on the main road, or working the bay as watermen, telling stories about how the Chesapeake is just about farmed clean every season by crabbers at the mouth or the headwaters leaving nothing left for those working the midland shoals.

This area hasn't changed much in one hundred years. It is like this everywhere, the coming and going of things. I can't imagine what my house would look like if left untouched. When I don't mow the lawn for a few weeks it looks like a refuge for timber wolves. But these trees weren't here a century ago and I sat on my porch and wondered if there had been other trees or if this land was barren, or was it used by the Powhatans, or was it home to some former slave family, or just a dumping ground. Evidence is scarce, buried beneath the roots of this small forest.

And Death Said

All of us will return to nature, somehow. I like to think that spending so much time there while alive will make it more familiar to me when I'm dead. Perhaps as the wind moves my ashes into the ages yet to come, I might think, "I remember this place; I've rested before in this place."

Practically speaking, how we are buried is nearly always tied to how we live.

Arlington Cemetery and most other military cemeteries command a respect for those interred there. They remain privileged for men and women who sacrificed so much, often everything, for their country. On foreign soil stand some cemeteries for soldiers who could not come home from war. Where we are buried or where our ashes are spread is indeed linked directly to how we lived our lives. "Location! Location! Location!" is the call for real estate whether above or below the surface.

I could be buried in Madagascar. There, every once in a while the people dig up their ancestors' bones and dance around with them to music at a party, and then re-bury them when they're done. Some ancient Chinese dynasties believed coffins should be closer to heaven to get there faster so they hung them from cliffs. One practice I'm not so keen about is strangulation. It seems in old-time Fiji, the loved ones of the deceased, including sons, would be killed as well so death wasn't such a lonely event.

I don't often think about my own eternal, motionless resting place and where I wish to spend the future of all futures. But if eternity doesn't start until life stops, at least I get the choice right now of where I get to hang out later; it is like making reservations. Do I want to go back to Brooklyn? I see no reason. A cemetery in Virginia somewhere seems convenient. I am very attached to the small town where I went to college in western New York and there is a beautiful cemetery there, but that's not convenient at all. The options are incredible. One can, with the right connections, be blasted into space, splattered on the moon, or buried at sea. Become a great statesman or writer and be buried at Westminster Cathedral. Run for and win the presidency and be buried at your own library in your own state in the room next to the replica of the Oval Office. Become a seminarian, then a priest, a bishop, cardinal and eventually the Pope, and be buried in St. Peter's where sainthood is not out of the question.

I could be cremated and have my ashes spread in a place of much significance. Maybe my relatives can shake my soot out the window of a Cessna above the Great South Bay. Better still, a colleague can buy some rolling papers and divvy me up among my students and let everyone smoke me. Small smoke rings can rise like empty words until the wind carries me away. If my family would foot the bill, I'd like one of those stone mausoleums with stained glass windows and candles for people to light, but it seems not just slightly pretentious. No, I like the idea of spreading my ashes aimlessly about some deep waterway or, better still, along a footpath in Spain where my own Camino can continue and continue. And then, like Whitman, "If you want me again look for me under your boot soles."

I'm not sure where I want to go when I go. Maybe that's why I write so much; so that the body becomes redundant. If we live well, death might just be irrelevant. And spending so much time in nature is, then, obvious. Our natural state is naked, outside, where all our needs, including shelter and food, are readily available.

Maybe so many people spend so little time in nature because it scares them, forces them to see just a little too far down that path.

As for me, maybe I'll simply go away. Relatives can scan maps years later and speculate, point at Spain or Mexico and say, "Yes, there. He is probably there. Perhaps," and their imaginations can skip to distant, romantic places. And like Virgil's personified "Death," I can twitch their ears and whisper, "Live . . . live now . . . I'm coming."

The Garden of Mediocrity

It is autumn and in the garden the peppers gave up for now, yielding enough to cover their cost, making them worthwhile, of course, for the fresh taste and the seasoning of satisfaction. The cucumbers, too, have let me know they're growing weary, pulling it together enough to hand over a few last small ones, but their withering leaves and the absence of new growth announce it's time for me to head to the stand in the village to get the vegetables. The tomatoes were the blowout. Early on I harvested bowls of cherry tomatoes, but they grew smaller and more tart, and now they seem to be spitting out just one or two here and there from behind brown vines, as if to say, "Wait, here's another. You might as well eat it here. No point in 'gathering' them." I haven't yet done the accounting on the tomatoes but in the end each one might have cost me more than I care to admit.

The eggplant win. I only had four plants, and one of them was behind what turned out to be a snake-sunning spot, but in the end, I harvested a comfortable amount of eggplants, and while I can only eat so much of the stuff, it is rewarding nonetheless, which is why a garden to begin with.

I like taking from the earth—harvesting fruit and finding soil beneath my fingernails, the dirt under my feet, the unmistakable aroma of tomato vines and cucumbers. I start the season with visions of baskets filled with big, ripe tomatoes, a row of peppers of various colors next to the bowl of string beans, which it turns out deer rather enjoy. Reality digresses from the virtual image, but I never tire of spending time in the heat and feeling the hot sun on my back. There is always a buzz of flies and the occasional sound of a bee, and when I go back inside I have a sense of abandonment if I don't get back there soon. And sometimes there are storms, downpours, but even in the rain—sometimes especially in the rain—I enjoy the peace, the absolute presence, of the garden as nature, controlled yet uncontrollable.

It gives so much more than fruit. I have worked in my mind on more than a few writing projects there, and worked out some worries, burying them forever beneath the mulch and compost. I enjoy the eternal sensation that I am gathering from the garden in a fashion not unlike Thom Jefferson, Voltaire, or Cicero, who said if you have a garden and a library, you have everything you need. I spend my Sundays out there not in conversation, but consultation with George Bernard Shaw who said, "The best place to find God is in a garden; you can dig for him there." And, of course, Monet, who said, "The garden is my most beautiful masterpiece." It is art. Writing is not unlike the work in the soil outside. The high hopes before starting, the impatience, the need to weed and prune (Hemingway must have done a lot of pruning), and water. If we give to the garden, it tells us stories, it feeds our imagination and seasons our lives, deliciously. Someday when I can no longer tend to the plants and vines, I'll long remember the sun on my neck and the feel of taking a tomato or cucumber off the vine and resting it gently in the basket, and then its sweet taste that afternoon.

And I hope the garden remembers me. I wonder if

someday when someone else clears out the area to garden, or even perhaps build, or plant grass, when someone has long impressed his own identity on this land, will some piece of me stay behind? Maybe someone will find an old rusty wire from the bean vines, or the rotted-out bottom of a basket I left too long in the soil one winter. Maybe someone will find herself humming a tune I left there in the spring air while turning over the ground for lettuce and squash. We try hard not to leave our mark in nature, allowing it to remain its trusted and pure self, but a part of me prays that if someone excavates the area that used to be "my" garden, she will find some inspiration.

Present Tense

The days following New Years are always the ones we inevitably balance by both looking back and looking ahead. We assess and dismiss and excuse and celebrate our actions and inactions from the last year, and we resolve to act and hold back in the year to come. It can be hard enough to do one of those things—recall and reignite—but both simultaneously is a juggling act which may make one's mind melt. To keep the goings and leavings intact, I walk outside where nature forgives my shortcomings and takes no issues with my plans.

I get up early by design. I like to listen to that pre-dawn stillness which in no time at all a thousand voices will disturb. I like the way the light holds off a while, almost as if it awaits my arrival to ask permission to spill across the sky. And then slowly the silence creeps off and hides behind some trees somewhere just before the phone rings, before the traffic picks up, before it is time to track time again. I spend some of the morning looking forward to the day and some of the day remembering, but mostly I prefer to simply be present as the sun comes up and the morning flock feeds behind the oyster boats on the bay.

The first lesson for me, then, of every single day is to simply be present; to rise deliberately like the sun, to allow my ritual to become fresh so that remembering and muscle memory are not necessary or desired.

But before the sun bends toward day, I set aside time on some trail for the sole purpose of revisiting my life as best I can recall. My memory is slipping a bit, and I find these moments in nature to be especially rewarding. They remind me I'm still alert enough to recognize the value in becoming me now, and it is a time to allow my emotions to take flight as they wish. I love how I can see clear as sunlight my father putting his fingers up to show me how much Scotch he wanted, the same amount every time. I love how I remember that so well I can still see him sitting there and hear him saying, "Just about this much, thank you" to the point I can't breathe. Some people go lifetimes without missing their dads, cursing them for convoluted reasons. I love how I loved and was loved so that now my eyes sting. Why would anyone not want to feel this way? Why would anyone wish to avoid the sadness that comes with good memories?

If I could take only one memory with me when I move into an age of forgetting, it would be walks to the river, my son on my shoulders, the sun on my back, those moments. Or the times we went fishing when he was four, never catching a thing and never caring. Or maybe the sound of house wrens just before dawn, or the whippoorwills just after dusk. I'd like to take that feeling of an open fire on my face and the cool night on my back. Or the sound of my father's voice telling me to sleep well. Or my mother's laugh, the way she takes a long breath. I'd like to forget all the times I got angry, all the times I was critical, and replace them with the memories of all the times I listened to the sound of rain on the canvas awning at our home when I was a child.

I know I'll want to remember one more time the fog-horns on the Great South Bay drifting through the air, my brother and sister still asleep, my mother making coffee, my father in his bed. I take it the grand design allows we forget the minutia as we age, but I'll salvage what I can. I like remembering the way my son laughed uncontrollably when he was two and I chased him across a field. Or the echo of the speakers at my high school football game, or the sound of cars off in the distance when my friends and I would hang out in someone's backyard or neighborhood street on a Friday night, laughing, telling stories about nothing at all.

Sometimes now when I am out for a walk, I stand at the water and wonder where everyone is. And I look up the coast and imagine my childhood friends, now adults, sitting with their families, reading the paper, watching a movie, most likely long ago forgetting what we did when we were young. But I'm glad they're there, just a few decades away, somehow still part of some shared history.

So, briefly I embrace melancholy; I celebrate memory. It is just that in the early morning, before the sun has had her say, before I am about to walk into the realm of a thousand voices and the movement of life, I like to remember that it's been a good ride so far. The length of a lifetime from the beginning looks nothing at all like the brevity of that life from the end, like standing on a diving board terrified to leap, knowing you have to for all the others lined up behind you waiting to have their chance. It's your turn, so you jump despite the fear of how far it is, but when you "rise again and laughingly dash with your hair," you look up at where you started and think, that wasn't so far at all.

No, it isn't far at all, which is why I like to remember early each day the view from the late afternoon, when shadows slide in almost without warning, and recollection is nearly required. I remind myself just after dawn, when the cardinals and Carolina wrens still spark about the woods, that it won't be long, not long at all.

The Murder of Crows

Albatross travel in rookeries. Alligators in congregations like old women with alligator purses at church picnics. It's a dazzle of zebras and a wisdom of wombats. A descent of woodpeckers might peck at a clat of worms, if a plump of wildfowl doesn't find them first. A pack of wolves remain a pack if they remain still, but once they move it's a rout. A pod of whales when swimming with a pod of walruses becomes a gam but will never swim with a hover of trout. It's true. A smack of jellyfish, a charm of hummingbirds, and a string of ponies will never, ever meet. Goats are a tribe, giraffes, predictably, a tower, and frogs an army.

But most people still call everything that flies a flock, that swims a school, and that runs on four legs a herd. It's a glint of goldfish and a band of gorillas, and a leash of greyhounds, which, because of no leash laws in the county where I live, often escape the rotten fence surrounding a neighbor's yard.

Deer move in herds, unless they're bucks then it's a brace, like ducks are when on the ground (as opposed to the flock in the sky or a raft of ducks in water). Eagles have a convocation, elk join gangs, falcons have a cast system, while emus show up in mobs. A caught fish is a catch but miss the big one and it remains in a draft, though more commonly a school, which really should be shoal, a word corrupted in the current of time. A bloat of hippos, a cackle of hyenas, a party of jays and a troop of kangaroos.

The mice in my son's closet are a mischief, the moles labor beneath a scourge of mosquitoes. Parrots are good company, and porcupines prickle; really, a prickle of porcupines. Raccoons gaze in a gaze, but it's an unkindness of ravens, which I suppose are a bit standoffish. Salamanders travel in a congress, which makes sense for their basic sliminess, but sharks, partly because they scare the crap out of us, move not in a school but a shiver. Vultures have a venue, and while kittens are a kindle, wild cats are a destruction. Go figure.

People. Well, people travel alone, or as a couple, a duo if performing. Add a bass player and it's a trio, one more makes a quartet, or a foursome on the greens. We move in gangs, we travel in groups unless we're after someone then it's a posse. We gather as an assembly, we make up one body, we are together the population, we are as a whole a society, we are as history a civilization. We started as two, tradition tells us, in a garden of wildlife, including a dule of doves but only one serpent.

Scientists estimate there are ten million species of organisms on earth, and they all have names. Today for lunch my son and I had oysters and clams raised in beds in a river. It was just the two of us, a couple of guys, until later when we joined a group of friends to move into a crowd of others which, when the oysters ran out, turned into a mob.

Tonight, I'll sit in peace on the porch and gaze at a galaxy of stars, completely alone.

Border Lines

In Arizona is a wildlife preserve called the Arizona-Sonora Desert Museum. It is wide open with wildlife roaming as if visitors were on the Serengeti. No sense of cages anywhere; no sense of imprisonment or danger. You can stand at the edge of a field and know with complete certainty the lions are not going to cross the abyss and attack, no matter how badly they may want to. Takes a little of the fun away, but at least it is safe.

Places like these have become not only common but standard; they are a means of protecting wildlife and helping save endangered species, as well as a means of educating us up close to the wildlife we otherwise would only see in movies; and they also displace the cramped and often unhealthy conditions which exist in some zoological parks around the country. Not all, but some are outdated and could benefit from the space that places like the Sonora Desert provide.

The most amazing aspect is the engineering. They figured out a way to create a barrier which blended naturally into the landscape yet is impenetrable. There is no need for cages or large chain linked, reinforced fences enclosing tight spaces. No walls are needed to separate us; they figured out how to use the landscape. I am not a fan of human-made objects in nature; the dangerous ones, of course, like fish hooks and soda pop cans and piles of garbage, but the innocent as well, such as dams and dikes and walls. The barriers at this museum make sense because you don't realize they are there. Think of the applications.

Still, I clearly remember wishing I was on the other side of the abyss. I wanted to walk around with the animals; it seemed so peaceful. I have always been drawn to animals, whether in nature, as pets, or at places like the Desert Museum.

On my own road which ends at a river are farms with alpacas, goats, sheep, and some horses. At one time someone even had yaks. I love the honesty and pureness of nature and animals; they simply "are." We humans keep changing; in fact, we change so much that "change" has become routine, predictable, almost expected. But in the natural world change comes in centuries, and animals' behavior is organic and brutally honest. As Byron once wrote, "I love not man the less, but nature more." I often feel safer in the wild among animals in their natural habitat than surrounded by humans instinctively feeling threatened in their constructed habitat. John Muir insisted that wilderness is a necessity; that there must be places for human beings to satisfy their souls.

I have always preferred the other side of where I am. In college I crossed the Niagara into Canada, in Arizona, crossing into Mexico was not simply a day off but a way to wander into another culture, another existence so diametrically different from how I was raised I couldn't help but be curious. Curiosity led to immersion. And once we do cross that abyss, work our way through the dangerous slopes and landslides which can keep us from trying, the landscape is welcoming and engulfing.

Nature shows us that what we are made of is determined by how we we handle our own tribulations. Some escape by running away, moving on; some have the courage and dynamic traits necessary to open up and expose the real struggle, and others build walls.

Some isolate themselves through complete extraction from a bad situation or avoid any possibility of danger to begin with. But all the things in life worth experiencing often involve risk. Often loss. Nature most notably. The fact is you can't reach for new heights unless you let go of something first. And to add one additional trite example to the mix, while Frost wrote the line, "Good fences make good neighbors," he was being ironic.

No. They don't. There is danger in letting down the guard, in opening up in front of strangers, in getting closer to the risks, but it is the only way to grow, the only way to understand who we are and where we go next. No journey—absolutely no journey—can possibly continue if we build walls.

3:30 pm

What time is it in your life?

If life happened in a day, and Einstein is horrifically more accurate than we would like, then let's make a six-am sunrise birth, and place death around a nine-pm sunset. I've always preferred summers for the extended daylight hours.

And if we break a life of ninety years (I'm an optimist) into a day, we live about six years an hour, or a year every ten minutes. Goes fast doesn't it? In fact, my clock reads 3:30 pm. School's out, lunch has been made, eaten, and cleaned up, and the morning hours are so long ago I barely recall them anymore.

If life happened in a day, or thought of another way, if life seemed to occur in units small enough to measure as such, we'd make sure we didn't miss much, no matter the weather or how tired we are. We'd call our closest companions and ask them to join us—we'd go through this together. *It is too bad we can't do this again*, we'd admit. *I don't want to miss any of it*, we'd say, suddenly aware of how fast time goes by, how many moments we let slip away. In fact, just talking about the fleeting morning might make us miss those hours of the day's youth when discovery is ripe and exploration is new. Those hours of life when no one but us has yet discovered the forest out back, the rapids in the creek down the road, or the view from the bent branches of a birch.

Looking back at my own day, around 10 am I lived in a yellow house next to a reservoir. It was a quaint village surrounded by a larger town, and across the street was a small post office and an antique store. Just up the winding road was an apple orchard where I bought bags of apples and where my neighbor the postmaster would buy me an apple pie for shoveling her driveway. I loved then, and I often talk about how I wish it was 10 am again, and I once again was leaving work to head to the mountain to hike to the summit to see kettles of hawks. Just an hour later, I was gone, living in a different latitude and finding myself finding myself once again. Love was easier than it should be and shorter than I had hoped, and the lessons learned so late in the morning stole my energy for a while. Exhaustion isn't always because of age; sometimes it is momentum. But time passes. I'd give the next six hours to have a few minutes back, but we can't. We must look forward. If I spend too much time regretting what happened at 11 this morning, I'll blow right through the afternoon without noticing the way the light of the sun can bring everything back to life.

At noon I walked to the river with my son on my shoulders, and we laughed our way through the early afternoon, hiking through woods and eventually continents. It was just about three this afternoon we trained across Siberia, and ten minutes later hiked across Spain. If my clock battery broke between three and four, I'd consider myself a lucky man. What a day it has been so far. I can't recall a single hour of my life I'd not do again. From sunrise on I've had a great time trying to stay one clip in front of the bend, with golden moments I couldn't have scripted myself. Maybe that's why the day seems so fast—I'm really having a great time.

Did you ever stop and just recall a moment from years ago like it had just happened, just now? I mean so that you can taste the meal and smell where you were, feel it, so real like it just happened, just now, but it didn't. That happened to me today, over and over and over, and now it is 3:30, and it is happening again. Thank God happy hour is so close; I need a drink.

Tonight, from 6 to 9, I'm going to take my time and do the best I can.

What time is it in your world?

In Humans

Scientists can now "edit" genes in a human embryo to prevent a disease. As a writer and a professor of writing I stand strongly behind any form of editing. It is, after all, an attempt to make something better either by adding clarity, eliminating awkwardness, or, in this case, correcting errors. It is difficult to find fault with this.

I know the arguments.

Gene manipulation of any sort can lead to "designer" babies. Sure, parents with money will be able to not only eliminate disease but order up some character traits not already fine-tuned in the sperm, while those without the means will suffer the process of natural selection and have to be satisfied with what God gave. Further, the embryo-envy group will insist that this could lead us into dangerous territory including cloning, or possibly creating a robot-like race.

Slow down.

There are regulatory speed-bumps still to overcome. In the meantime, if we can scrape the cancer out of a kid why would we not want to? And when someone suggests it really should be "God's will" how the baby comes out, I get frustrated, pissed off, and downright angry. My reactions all are traits that could have been removed with one more run through of gene-check when I was born. But how can anyone not become infuriated? It is God's will that children be born with cancer? Cerebral palsy? Cystic fibrosis? Seriously? If so, if those elements should not be screwed with because they were pre-determined, then how (in God's name) do these people not know it possibly was God's will to enable scientists to finally have this moment where in some lab somewhere someone sat back, looked up and stared straight ahead, blinked, and said, softly to herself, "Praise God. We did it"? Under the acutely pretentious mentality that it was "God's will" that misfortune remain standard, we should have no medicines, eye glasses, or deodorant. You can't have it both ways; the same God that "allows" tragedy to befall a newborn might just have balanced His intent with a scientist's capability to solve the problem.

If some baby has a dangling modifier or comma splice, I say have at it. Eliminate the gene that bends toward polio, Chron's, leukemia, or blindness. Clean up the embryonic paragraph which begins with an incomplete digestive system, a fragmented spine, a misspelled heart valve. And, my dear scientists, surgeons, or managing editors—however you will be so labeled—while you're in there, quickly skim through the frontal lobe and fine-tune the common sense. See what you can do about the math scores on SATs and the gene that enables tail-gating, stealing, lying, and pain. This little move toward disease control could be a step toward babies designed to share with others, to empathize, to help the needy and to not text and drive.

I wonder, though, if personality traits can be manipulated as easily as cancer control. If so, can we finally make a move toward understanding and compassion? Is it possible that this discovery is the end to the common trend toward gluttony and greed? These designer babies might, by design, be intolerant of hunger, might make it a crime to be homeless because of some doctor who checked the fetus galley sheets and noticed a gene which still allowed unnecessary suffering and had the presence of mind to grab a bottle of amniotic white-out.

In a world where so many have no issue with the swerve toward technology and computers that think ahead, robots with limbs not unlike our own, what is so wrong with a step toward humanity? Instead of improving machines to help us make life more convenient and comfortable, how about making the technology obsolete by improving the people?

How much embryonic manipulation will it take before hunger is no longer an issue? How many edits is it before the desire for war doesn't even enter someone's mind?

People must stop being suspicious of science and finally understand that humanity is dying; we are on a slow decline and have become more accustomed to crude comments than constructive conversation, indifferent toward arms buildup and troop movement, and infinitely more blasé about hope, possibility, and peace. When did we decide that disease and suffering were simply part of humanity and will never change?

Still not convinced that gene-manipulation might be worth investigating further just to understand the possibilities? Than ask yourself this: If you knew your child was going to be born with a painful disease or perhaps die at ten years old from cancer, and you could stop it from happening, would you?

It is What it is

I love every season. I like the icy winds on my face and equally enjoy the dripping heat of the deep south. Nature is objective; she just lays it out there on the line and says, "Today, you're going to freeze your ass off," but means nothing by it. It is absolute honesty. It does not differentiate between those who love the cold and those who don't. The same was true in the Sonora Desert; it wasn't unusual to hike in 110-degree heat, but it was what it was. Sometimes, even, nature will whisper, "Then go inside if I'm too hot for you."

That's what draws me to nature; it keeps me in the moment, I experience again what humans have experienced since the dawn of us. But these days surrounded by processed landscapes and prepackaged cities, people tend to pass judgement on everything from lip gloss to the definition of genocide; they categorize and change their minds; their moods can be unpredictable and hard to trust. This isn't the case in nature. Nature just might be the only place of absolute fairness. It doesn't bully. It doesn't ridicule or praise. It simply doesn't care; which is all that is necessary for one to be oneself. And there is more than enough in nature for me to be myself. Ray Bradbury was right: There is more than enough here to fill me; there will always be more than enough.

It's why I walk. Cinder block hallways and poster-laden classrooms offer nothing. When I am in the woods or near water, the criticism is all internal and ironically it is only at that point it is mostly positive. I am proud of myself when out there, first for being out there, for shedding the residue of concrete expectations. And what I find when the sun is sliding along the water or the leaves linger just a few moments more before letting go for good, is that I expect more out of myself than I do when I am closed in. In the hallways and meeting rooms and online spaces saturating the air with invisible communication cables, I do what is necessary, sometimes what I think is more than necessary, but always I am tethered by others exceedingly low expectations. But when I'm out on my own meandering I tear down the low-bar mentality and realize what I am capable of.

And it occurs to me that since I do my best in those situations, I should spend more time in those situations.

The view from my wilderness is almost always internal, clothed in the spectacular colors and soft breezes of nature. When I walk along a deserted road I take full responsibility for every thought and action and reaction. When I stroll down the oceanfront or along the river I can find the right words, discover the correct image. I remember what I think about when out there. It stays with me, whereas the conversations in corridors are often little more than white noise.

It isn't only that nature doesn't pass judgement on my decisions or actions that relaxes me and allows some sort of organic process to work at its best; it is that I can clear my head of those who do.

Awake. Right. Now.

I fell through the ice on a frozen lake in northern Norway. It was two in the morning, twenty below, and I followed two friends across the snowy ice toward a road on the other side. I heard the ice crack and I stood still, a green band of aurora borealis bent just above us, and I stood still like Wile E. Coyote—suspended for just a moment listening to the ice crack—and thought, "oh, wow, shit," and went through.

I landed just about ten inches below the surface on another ice shelf. I stood just deep enough for frigid water to cover and fill my boots about calf-high. I waited for the next crack when Joe turned and we froze in fear of us both plunging into the lake. This wasn't the first time I'd walked on thin ice, but previous mishaps were mostly metaphorical. I stood with icy feet; my heart pounded in my chest ready to plunge into my stomach when the ice again cracked. Nothing.

Our friend John turned and laughed. "It's day melt," he said, ahead of us by twenty feet, already on the shore. "The surface ice melts a bit each day then freezes at night, but it's thin. That's what we were walking on. The second layer you landed on is probably six feet thick."

"Why didn't you go through?" I asked. John was six feet, two inches and not a light man.

"I was first," he said. "I loosened it for you."

I sloshed to shore, took off my socks, and stood at the end of a fjord when across a field, six moose stood taller than us all. I put my boots back on and watched the moose move toward us. They were bull-like, each one heavier than the three of us combined. The night was still, and the air was calm. To the north lay nothing but wilderness for a thousand miles; the Arctic Circle sat a hundred miles south. This was as close to sacred ground as I ever got. I was soaked in below zero temperatures, green bands of borealis bent above my head, the moose moved toward us, and I never felt so awake, like sleep wasn't part of the Human idea, like caffeine was a tranquilizer. Awake. The northern lights lingered like they were in water, as if the the sky was submerged and the green bands couldn't bend faster than the deep blue flow would allow, and we floated between. The moose moved closer. I held my breath. Two leaped just beyond our reach and bounced over the ice with absolute grace.

That moment, right then, will never go away. Only nature gives us this.

We rise every morning and gaze at life around us, but how often are we awake, I mean completely and blatantly alive? Studies tell us that most of us sleep a third of our lives and most of us work a third of our lives. And now at my age with hopefully about a third of my life left, I'd like to spend as much of what amounts to one third of that third being fully awake before the ground falls beneath my feet.

From This Green Hill

Not all of nature is natural. Sometimes we interrupt the pastoral for reasons more permanent than nature herself.

Recently I was at Arlington National Cemetery and stood near a small wall on a tranquil hillside, and I could see Washington, D.C., the Washington Monument and other memorials to our founding fathers.

The unobstructed view looks out upon our nation's capital, where for almost 250 years some of these souls have challenged the balance of power. A few of our former leaders lie just feet from this unassuming spot: an eternal flame for John F. Kennedy, a small cross for his brother Robert and, for their older brother, Joseph, one of the hauntingly familiar headstones. Across these green fields in all directions stand thousands upon thousands of marble markers, all carefully carved with the names of veterans and spouses, their birth and death dates, battalion or division and rank and conflict, a cross or a star, variations of both. A flag.

From this protected promontory I could see century-old oaks. Magnolias and dogwoods shrouded headstones like commanders keeping their soldiers safe. The Tomb of the Unknowns, mausoleums, small, singular sarcophagi and miniature monolith monuments stood scattered across acres of fields of fallen men and women who once stood as strong as those very stones that mark their last battle.

From this green hill I could see wildlife. I watched brave birds feed at an arm's length away and then scatter to the safety of a nearby branch. Starlings perched upon headstones, and striking red cardinals gazed from the low branches of a tall maple. It was theirs, once, as were all the battlefields and all the cemeteries from Winchendon, Massachusetts, to the Texas Coastal Bend, before these battles took their toll, and men—boys—were buried in this wilderness.

From this tear-soaked soil I could see Vietnam, its rivers and forests where death kept too close to birth, whose beauty and wilderness taught men to pray and made brothers of them all. I could see the village battles between unknown enemies and blameless boys who should have been home riding bikes and reading books. I could see the more than fifty-thousand Americans never to become authors or professors, scientists or librarians, gathered beneath this field where their legacy is our common charge.

Beyond the Potomac, I could see Korea, the Philippines and New Guinea. The voices of spouses still crying for a husband to come home, women, standing alone too young, holding the small hands of children starting their fatherless flights toward tomorrow. I could see the medals and markers, veterans hugging veterans above a brother's eternal assignment, saying, "It should have been me." "He gave it all." "He saved my life." "He was too young."

From this hallowed ground I could see Normandy. I could see the parachutes falling under the cover of night. I could see rows upon rows of men who marched side by side through shallow, blood-filled, mine-laden water toward the only hope left. I could see the hillside and the secured toehold. I could see the American flags on Omaha Beach and Utah Beach. I could see the graves of those forever beneath foreign soil and the ships returning with thousands of heroes.

I could hear taps, the prayers of priests, the commanders' thank-yous, the nation's solace.

From this sacred spot I could see into France, the sacrificial fields, the trenches that saved the lives of our great-grandfathers. I could see the muddy, barren no-man's land where brave men crossed only to lie here, now, beneath crosses too many to mention.

From this vantage I could see the heirs of Lexington and Concord. I could see Saratoga and Yorktown. I could see the battle for freedom, the commitment to integrity, the promise to defend. I could see the fight for the greater good. From this spot on a green hill I could see a small group of men standing like stone walls against England and claiming with absolute clarity and without compromise that we will be free. We will stay free. We will not fail.

From that green hill, from that perspective on such honorable sacrifice, I could see what bought our freedom. I could count the crosses, the sum of which cannot be measured, whose cost cannot be calculated.

News Cast Off

This past Sunday morning I listened to the news while I drove home from a village across the river. No wonder I am on blood pressure medicine.

I turned into the driveway and wound my way through the four hundred feet of woods to the house and remained outside all afternoon. I found myself in desperate need of a little peace of mind. It seems the seasonal changes in nature are the only persistent and predictable aspects of life. When I am in the woods or walking along the water, I could as easily be ten years old. I could be on Long Island, or in central Massachusetts, or here at home, finishing off a cup of tea on the porch as wrens come and go for safflower seed.

Yesterday the sky looked like it might snow though it was in the fifties. It had that low gray layer of late autumn haze out over the bay so that I could look right at the sun. It was pale yellow, almost a mere shadow of a glow. Just a few days ago the sky was so deep blue it was as if there couldn't possibly be a storm anywhere in the hemisphere; one of those days. As far across the bay as I could see, and to the west up the river, nothing. Not a single disturbance moved the water or the trees or even the marsh-reeds, which tend to bend at the slightest brush of breeze even when a heron takes flight.

So I stayed outside all day yesterday. Mostly I raked,

but I also moved planters around, piled empty pots behind the garden shed, and cleared off the trail in the back woods where deer bed down at night, and at dusk a fox always scurries around waiting for leftovers tossed in the brush. The oaks are nearly bare, except for a few that keep their leaves until spring. This land has mostly hardwoods, so the view above isn't impeded anymore, but down at eye level an abundance of holly keeps the property green all year. The laurel, as well, remains, and a little higher up the thin pines stay green.

It might snow this year. It seems every year snow falls more regularly. Three years ago, it snowed so much I don't remember it clearing out enough to see the grass until well into February or March, which for this part of Virginia out on the Chesapeake is unusual. I'll take it, or the heat, doesn't matter. Ice cold hands from doing work without gloves or a back covered in sweat in August are equally satisfying. I like being in nature, wearing it, letting it penetrate beyond the visual so that all my senses come to life.

From my perspective in these woods, whether the view be unobstructed across fields and waterways, or blocked, able to see only the nearby thicket like shadows on the wall of a cave, it is a beautiful world; despite the news today, we live in a beautiful world. While humanity votes in and casts out, the natural world bends and turns and spins and thrusts itself forward in endless revolutions of perpetual next. Our world is still an infant, despite what we call history as well as histrionics. It teethes on change and feeds on self-indulgence. To be fair, it always has.

But *this* country, where the river has ebbed and flowed for tens of thousands of years, and the watermen still cross the reach each day before dawn like their great-grandfathers did, is stronger than any news cycle. Here in the early morning a channel marker rings and the oyster boats return to their docks by the time the morning news anchors have poured their first cup of coffee and sign on to keep us informed about what is "important."

I have no argument in nature. I have no sense of conflict. The paths are not compromised by a lack of decorum, the deer are not prone to an absence of character, and the osprey and eagles which frequent these skies do not suffer from questionable integrity. Nature is neither crass nor belittling; it does not lie. The trees remain firm in their convictions, the birds—with one exception—do not mock other birds, and the skies, whether cloudy or clear, have no ulterior motives.

What Mahatma Said

I'm in search of simplicity, of those perfect moments we normally only experience with people we love. You know the ones—laughing with someone so hard that just recalling that moment makes you laugh again; a deep conversation over a glass of wine about the beauty of simplicity, the meaning of it all. Maybe you go for a walk and there's a soft breeze; maybe you sit on the porch and there are a million stars, or maybe just a gentle rain falling on the awning and the sound is as eternal as a sigh. Those moments when what was and what will be are shrouded by the widening love of that moment. Those times. We live for those times.

Of course, we can't always live in the moment. We remember and plan by nature, and the need to survive requires lessons and anticipation. But the art of being mindful of the now is slipping away. We are engrossed in connections. Distraction has crept into our lives like a slowly rising tide, soaking the moments normally set aside for a little peace of mind. We check the phone, get online, get absorbed by news updates, protests, uprisings, the falling Dow, we jump at the "bing," worry about what didn't get done, worry about what might happen. We used to let go and simply "Be," but we now hold on, afraid of missing something, believing we need to keep up, stay informed. There is always—always—human sound streaming from somewhere, and it is rarely laughter. Hell, even tears would do if it meant a moment of honesty. But instead it is a video, music, conversations, the press, the pressing need to know, the pressure of parenthood, of teenagehood, of the extraordinary task of having an ordinary day.

I don't have a solution, I really don't. I don't know what to tell you. It simply is an observation.

As for me, I'll walk the water's edge and think about walking the water's edge. I'll talk to a friend and share some wine and laugh about what strikes us, have deep conversations about what sets our souls on fire, and then try and keep it burning well into what's next. I have a few symptoms of this chronic condition called "time." My wrist hurts for no reason at all; I have memory issues; I listen to a lot of Van Morrison. Still, I am fine with all that; it is like the proctor calling out from the front desk that there are only thirty minutes left to finish the exam: it makes me sit up and get down to business. And it helps me focus on simplicity and the moment I'm in. One of the advantages of trying to focus on the "now" is I don't really need too much memory to do that anyway. All I need is a place to walk.

I'm wondering more and more lately if there are any Mother Theresas alive and well, any Schweitzers, any Kings or Gandhis. It certainly doesn't feel like it. In the years between my birth and turning ten, we saw the initiation of the Peace Corps, Earth Day, NASA's moon launch, the Civil Rights Act, and more, including idealistic events like Woodstock. It is hard to find hope now. It is difficult to put a finger on possible solutions. I understand the world was a bit too idealistic in a time that also brought us so many riots, the Vietnam War, assassinations of heroes, and more. But just a little more idealism wouldn't be so bad, would it?

I spend most of my time near water; maybe because of its constant unpredictability; maybe because of how true it is. It is cleansing; it is purifying. I really am finding it difficult to believe in much else anymore. Thoreau said there is a subtle magnetism in nature which if we unconsciously yield to will direct us right. I so yield.

But when I look out I remember what Gandhi said: "You must not lose faith in humanity. Humanity is like an ocean; if a few drops of the ocean are dirty, the ocean does not become dirty." And that sea, once it casts its spell, Cousteau once commented, holds one in its net of wonder forever.

Clarity

This morning a heavy mist settled on the ocean, turned the sky and horizon and breakers right up to the sand all one color, one dimension, like the façade on a movie set or some impressionistic painting. At the water's edge, I could see maybe thirty or forty feet before the wall of blue blocked my view. A group of pelicans flew by, inches above the calm ocean not far from where I stood, and about six or so dolphins moved past, their backs rising out; only one, just once, breached the water. Had she been another ten feet beyond I probably wouldn't have been able to watch.

It is winter, but it is warm, and no one is around, not the usual walkers, not the scattered homeless. It is quiet, and I walk at the water's edge in the salty air enjoying the peace. There is such a difference between the solitude through the day when I go for a walk or sit on a porch, and the peace found in nature where certain sounds, like gentle waves lapping the shore or an occasional call of a gull, remind me of the silence, force me to focus on what I'm not hearing. It reminds me of John Cage's, "4'33" which is that length of time of complete silence—a CD with a more-than-four-minute track of absolute nothingness; he makes the listener completely aware of the absence of sound. Walking along an empty coast early before the sun comes up, or, like this morning, when there simply is no sun to speak of, reminds me first of the peace I can count on to find there, and second of the noise I encounter when I move on.

Isn't there such a disturbing difference between quiet and peace? When I catch myself falling into some semblance of depression or confusion, I know I can clear my head. It is empowering to truly understand that when things are not going well I can walk to the water's edge, to the one spot I have found which has never changed and has never abandoned me, and let the salty air and ocean breezes clear away the confusion.

The problem, of course, is the ocean is not a cure; it is a bandage. After a while, the only remedy is to abandon society completely and camp out just this side of the high-water mark. No, one must address the cause of the need for escape. Ah, what an easy, Psych 101 response! Yes, the cause—it is an argument, a misunderstanding, a failure, a crossroads, a judgement, a realization, a loss too unbearable to contemplate. Yes, okay, it is one of those or maybe something else, it really doesn't matter. Because what so many do not understand about "escape" is that the "cause," no matter how solvable, no matter how seemingly simple, is often a permanent presence in one's soul created by a sense of abandonment and indifference, and it seems like there is no remedy, because often there simply isn't.

I have known people like this who could not escape; I have been close to people who found no recourse, could not negotiate the shadows, the parts of life without a clear and obvious path. One friend killed himself (and his dog) in his garage. A close colleague hanged herself in her kitchen. We all have a story; we all know some poor soul who never understood a way out.

There should be high school classes designed to help

students find peace. We should give college credit for lessons in perspective and escape.

Some seek therapy to talk it through, some medicate for balance, and some simply live in the middle, safe, where they never experience extremes, where highs and lows all wash out. And some go for walks, discover the beauty inside which cannot be shrouded by others' dismissal, by others' judgements. They put on some John Cage and escape to the water's edge where they can find themselves at peace somewhere out past the horizon, and they recall the words of the Dalai Lama: "Do not let the behavior of others destroy your inner peace."

And now it's late and I'm still a stone's throw from the ocean listening to the crashing waves. It's a warm night, and the tide is low so a walk at the water's edge keeps me far from the busy boardwalk and music-filled cafés. No one else is out here, and the light from the moon makes it easy to see where I'm going. I've been walking an hour. Some nights it takes longer than others to slow down my mind and clear my head. I heard once that if you spend enough time near the ocean you can hear it as far away as Nebraska. This must be true. Even in college, six hundred miles and thirty-five years away I seemed to sense when the water was like glass or choppy, or, like tonight, smooth with four-foot waves coming to shore in sets of three. There's a light wind.

No man is ever alone on the sea, Hemingway wrote. Over the years it has become for me a safe place to be. Ironic, really, when I stand at night close enough for my feet to get wet and face east, and the dark and distant horizon seems unforgiving. When I was seventeen I stood here looking out toward Spain, thinking about the reach, contemplating the journey. We all have that one place where we know all we need to know; where we have more than can ever be necessary. I don't have the science to explain the currents and I can't remember the names of the seabirds. But when a dolphin breaches the surface I have all the information necessary to satisfy why I'm out here to begin with: to slow down my mind and clear my head. The irony of my life as a college professor is I feel less isolated in nature than I do on campus.

People need to shake hands more, ask each other where they're from, where they're going. We need to stand in hallways laughing, building possibilities on the backs of anecdotes. It should take a while to get the room to quiet down. I shouldn't have to suggest people look up from their laps. We are on the edge of a dangerous change, and I fear if we're not careful, our efforts to be connected will cut us off completely.

Isolation is killing growth and suffocating ideas. And this great migration toward absolute individualism is rampant. People along the boardwalk take selfies instead of asking someone to take a picture, where in the process they might talk about where to eat, where to explore. Students sit before class in deep online conversations with friends they've known since seventh grade instead of finding out how the people around them might be part of their future, part of changing what's next and what can be. I have lost interest in this regressive approach to life—I hesitate to call it life.

Life is the way we make eye contact and understand each other; life is the stories we share of the times we laughed so hard it hurt. Life has depth and can't be communicated in memes or posts. It is about character, not characters; it is about making connections, not being connected.

So I come here and walk in seeming complete contradiction to my disdain for such growing isolation. But out here life is entirely visceral. The sand and the mist and the quiet distant call of a gull is primal and ancient and eternal. The waves are gaining strength and the tide has turned. By morning the water will be choppy, and the gulls will feed on schools of fish being chased by dolphins, and it will fill my mind with such peace I long to share it, to gather my friends and sit on blankets and watch the daily repetition of miraculous life.

But I can't find a soul.

Letting Go of Small Hands

We don't play with the kids enough. We don't walk on the grass enough, we worry too much about losing. We don't throw the ball enough, hike through the woods, climb the low trees, go out on a limb, eat fruit off the vine. We don't tell enough stories, listen to records, read enough poetry. It is one of the ancient arts, Mary Oliver reminds us. "It began as did all the fine arts; within the original wilderness of the earth."

We don't call old friends who are hard to find, aunts and uncles who made us laugh, stay longer with our parents talking about the times we had, talking about the rain. Being quiet. We don't journey enough to places close by, we don't find beauty in what there is plenty of, we don't appreciate what is common, we don't celebrate what is in our grasp. We've lost the art of solitude, of fasting, of quiet walks. Work isn't "life" but solely a means of sustaining life. Life is the way we sit around and laugh till two. Life is the feet on the coffee table, the tie undone, the kids asleep in their beds. Life is the sound of water in a pool, the sound of tea poured into china cups, the sound of distant thunder at dusk. Life is unwrapped gifts, cards in the mail, the smell of bacon on Sunday morning; drinking beer with friends on Friday night, the first cold day in autumn we need to wear a sweater, life is the spring grass showing beneath the melting snow. It's the mother in the door waving to her child moving away. It's the father at the observation deck waving to his son on the plane. It's the letting go of small hands; it's the giving away of the bride, it's the days that pass without a phone call, without a text message, without an interruption. Life is the distance between a falling leaf and the ground.

Epilogue

This time of year, when leaves start to fall, I recall a line I wrote which to this day bothers me: "Life is the distance between a falling leaf and the ground."

I loved that line. I was walking around home some years ago and it popped in my head. At the time I had been working on a piece called "Walled In" and the end of the essay digresses into a litany of "life is" comments. In fact, the last short page before this is an excerpt from the end of "Walled In." In it, I re-added the last line of the piece, which tied back to the narrative about stepping away from society a la Thoreau. The *Southern Humanities Review* picked up the piece and when I received the final edits before press I wrote Dan Latimer, the editor at the time, and asked him to strike the last line. He did.

I am pretty sure it isn't original. I googled it; I turned it in to turnitin.com; I tried everything. I don't read that much so I looked through the few possible books where I might find it, but nothing. I looked through poetry books, I called writers I know who do read books and asked them. I even, thinking it might have been in a passage read by a writer as a guest on NPR's "Fresh Air," wrote the show asking if anyone there, namely host Terry Gross, remembered the line. They were nice enough to write back politely suggesting I might be having a mental breakdown.

Paul McCartney to this day is not convinced he is the author of the music for "Yesterday." Unlike McCartney, I chose to strike the line. The piece went on to other outlets and has done very well through the years, sans line. I was concerned someone would recognize it and know it wasn't original, even though I'm pretty sure it is. My journalism training, however, requires me to be one hundred percent sure. "If you can't back up your sources," Dr. Jandoli repeated, "you don't have a story."

That might be in part why I slid away from journalism and into something more personal. I do not like fact-checking. Instead, I found stories in nature. Writers never stop working. Either some digressive thought about an ongoing work, or a new work, or a very old work, crawls into our consciousness while we are walking, or some quick phrase catches our attention and we know it is the beginning of or end of or transition to something. It is not on purpose; there is no attempt to blend writing and "life." I swear. It just happens. We are always working. An artist's brain functions differently. A photographer goes for a walk and finds himself framing nature, a painter sees color schemes, a musician notices sounds, and writers, well, complete mental breakdowns from information overload is not out of the question. It is why we despise the comment: "You know what you should write about?" Go away. Did you really think we were sitting around thinking "I have no idea what to write about, I hope someone makes a suggestion"?

And we don't actually "find" something to write about; it seeps into our existence like humidity or allergies. For me, I walk in the woods, or along the water, and the nature of nature is non-judgemental, absent of debate. I can walk for hours and my thoughts move through unattached to some human-inspired "suggestion" from a billboard or odd structure. It is organic, like leaves falling: thoughts let go and gather around.

Near my home at the river is a small strip of beach which changes with the weather and storms. Sometimes there is room enough to walk quite a way along the water, and other times the river moves right to the edge of the swamp or rip rap and to continue means wading through the tide. In either case, I am always discouraged at my inability to communicate the perpetual reality of that tide, the infinite days the water will ebb and flow, and the significance of nature compared to the miniscule roll I play in this short span of decades.

I don't even try. I stand back and let it all be. And the passing of time is enough sometimes.

That's writing. A writer spends a great deal of time not writing. Not because we have nothing to write about, but because we have an absolute conviction we can never, ever do it justice, and we are all too aware that we are never quite finished, or we have said all we can, and that life really is the distance between a falling leaf and the ground.

About the Author

Bob Kunzinger is the author of eight collections of non-fiction, and has been widely published in publications such as *World War Two History*, *Southern Humanities Review*, the *Washington Post*, the *St. Anthony Messenger*, and more, including notations for essays in *Best American Essays*. He lives and writes in Virginia.